100 healthy desserts

THE BIGGEST LOSER

100 healthy desserts

Delicious recipes for healthy living

NUTRITION CONSULTANT: DR TRENT WATSON

hardie grant books
MELBOURNE • LONDON

Contents

Introduction

THE BIGGEST LOSER IS ALL ABOUT CHALLENGING YOURSELF!

Secrets from successful Losers highlight how vital it is to find tasty low-fat, low-calorie foods that will help you in your weight-loss journey. Healthy eating doesn't need to be difficult – and The Biggest Loser – 100 Healthy Desserts *aims to make it even easier. With nutritious, delicious and easy-to-prepare recipes, it's a breeze to keep your weight in check. And, if you're planning on losing a few extra kilos, the recipes will help you to get back to a healthy weight range – so you can start enjoying a fuller life.*

To keep the weight off long-term there are some key habits that will increase your likelihood of being a winner:

KEY HABITS

- Exercise regularly.
- Eat breakfast.
- Follow a low-fat diet (this means lean meat, low-fat dairy products, low-fat cooking techniques, lots of vegetables, salad and fruit).
- Avoid fatty take-aways and fast food.
- Avoid weekend calorie blow-outs.
- If you have a bad day or a bad patch, start your weight-loss challenge again, as soon as you can.
- Weigh yourself regularly (but not obsessively!) and keep a record of your weight.
- Jump on small weight gains sooner rather than later, before they turn into big weight rebounds.

The Biggest Loser – 100 Healthy Desserts is designed to complement your weight-loss plans, whether you are using The Biggest Loser Club online, seeing an Accredited Practising Dietitian, using a commercial club or going it alone. In getting started, enlist the support of family, friends or work mates.

HOW DO YOU LOSE WEIGHT?

Do you want the honest answer? With commitment, hard work and a positive attitude: an attitude that means you forgive yourself when you experience setbacks and get right back up to continue on your journey. On a physical level, there are two ways of losing weight: eat less or exercise more, or both. To lose weight, you must create an energy deficit – that is, you need to consume less food (energy) than you actually use. You need to eat fewer kilojoules or calories than your body needs to get through the day; this way, your body will use its energy stores to make up the energy deficit.

Understanding this is the basis of successful weight loss, but clearly there's more to it than that, otherwise few people would be overweight. Your mind is the key – you have to really want to lose weight and you have to deal with all the blocks your mind puts in the way. Successful weight loss is all about attitude. What gets you up in the morning early so you can go for a walk? A positive can-do attitude and being organised by having clothes by your bed. What helps you forgive yourself when you eat too much? A positive attitude and an ability to recognise that one setback doesn't mean you have blown everything.

TO SUCCEED IN YOUR WEIGHT LOSS, YOU WILL NEED TO:

- accept yourself and where you are right now
- understand what triggers you to overeat
- break bad habits and learn new ones
- develop a strategy for bouncing back from setbacks
- learn positive self-talk
- recognise that an all-or-nothing attitude does not help your weight loss
- be responsible for, and accountable to, yourself
- change your lifestyle.

CHANGING YOUR BEHAVIOUR

Eating a nutritionally balanced diet and exercising are the keys to long-term weight loss. This isn't a new idea, yet it remains challenging for many people. Why? Because we make poor choices that over time become bad habits, which we then find hard to change. While your current habits and lifestyle have brought you to this point, it has happened over a long period of time. To lose weight, you need to recognise that it will take time to unlearn those habits and develop new responses, so that eventually you will have a new set of habits that support your new healthy lifestyle. Imagine if you decided you wanted to race the 400 metres at the Olympics, but you'd only just started training.

You would make a long-term goal and understand that it would take time, commitment and perseverance. You wouldn't expect to achieve it in a month, nor would you give up when you lost your first race or had your first injury. It is the same with changing your behaviour to lose weight.

Change is always challenging, and successful change takes time. It also depends on your stage of acceptance for taking action. You might be ready to change, you may still be deciding whether change is worth it or you may be preparing to change. Perhaps someone has bought you this book, but you do not think you need to change at all. Sometimes it's hard to accept that we have a health problem. We ignore it, procrastinate about it or simply deny its existence. Take the time to decide if you are ready. If you are, then it's time to plan, prepare and then act, recognising that the journey takes time. First are some ideas for modifying your behaviour.

Change one habit at a time

A total overhaul is likely to be too much too soon. You don't have to change everything at once. Do it step by step – commit to one new habit first and wait until it feels like second nature before committing to the next habit. Commit to being active for 30 minutes five days a week, or to reducing your fat intake by cutting out the hot chips at lunch, or to cutting down your alcohol intake to twice a week, or to getting up 20 minutes early so you can prepare a healthy lunch to take to work. By choosing to focus on one new habit at a time, you make the goal achievable, you'll become more confident as you achieve it and you'll be ready for the next step.

Start small

A dramatic change won't last. You already know this. Small changes make a difference – even just reducing your portion sizes and switching to water or diet drinks will lower your kilojoule intake. Making a small change in your lifestyle is manageable and will inspire confidence in yourself to make more.

Make one change that will have the most effect

If you're starting by making one change, choose to change the one habit that will make the most difference to your health. If you want to reduce the amount of sugar you eat, don't cut out the cake you have once a week, cut out the can of soft drink you have every day with lunch.

Be patient

You didn't gain weight in a week, so you can't expect to lose it in a week. Don't be in a hurry and don't give up when you fall back into an old habit – remember, you're still learning. It takes time and perseverance, and it's completely normal not to get it right straight away.

Be consistent

Modifying behaviour successfully is all about consistency. You need to replace bad habits with good habits, created through repetition. Commit to creating good habits daily. The more consistent you are, the faster you'll reach your goal. The less consistent, the longer it will take.

Be aware

Eating is often done without thinking – it's mindless. Start to become aware of what and when you eat. Practise eating with mindfulness – that is, pay attention to what and how much you are eating, and what you're doing at the same time. This gives you a chance to learn what triggers your overeating. Do you always reach for food after you've spoken to your mother? Do you always eat when you're watching TV? You need to start by breaking the habit. Speak to your mother when there's no food around; make a rule that you don't eat in front of the TV. Make it a rule that you don't eat when you're on the move or when you're doing something else. Focus on the food in front of you and pay attention to what you are eating.

Manage your environment

It's difficult to change your behaviour if nothing else changes. Making your home health-friendly will help you create and stick with your new habits.

As well as your home environment, manage other eating occasions. Eating healthily doesn't mean you can never eat out or get take-away. This is a lifestyle, not a diet of deprivation. The secret is planning ahead – what's the healthiest take-away you can get? Can you have a healthy snack before you go out to dinner? Any support you can give yourself in learning new behaviours will help make them your habits.

Change your thinking

Good food and exercise are just as vital for our mental wellbeing as our physical wellbeing – our state of mind drives our choices and influences our decisions. Generally, the healthier you are, the more positive your mental outlook will be and the less likely you'll be to engage in unhealthy habits. When everything is going well, it's easy to be positive but when things go pear-shaped we can often descend into a spiral of self-doubt, fear and uncertainty. Our confidence takes a knock and, once this happens a few times, it can quickly become a habit.

Negative thoughts are a self-fulfilling prophecy. Pay attention to your attitude to yourself and to your life. Listen to what you're thinking and what you're telling yourself. How do you talk to yourself? How much negative self-talk is happening in your head? Your internal dialogue affects how you feel, what you believe, and how you behave. Be aware of your negative self-talk and stop it as soon as you hear yourself. It can take time to create new positive thinking patterns and it's easy to slip back into old negative self-talk; when you find yourself being negative, laugh at the thoughts, tell yourself they're not true and replace them with the positive alternative.

Avoid using 'should' statements, over-generalising and all-or-nothing thinking. Choose a positive attitude and start believing in yourself now, as hard as it may feel; don't wait to lose 2, 10 or 30 kilograms before feeling good about yourself. Be proud that you are actively changing your life rather than just wishing for change. Remember what you like about yourself and what you are good at. Change your self-talk – start talking to yourself as you would a friend. Be caring, sensitive, understanding and friendly. You achieve nothing by putting yourself down. You are your first and most important supporter, and your support is vital in your effort to lose weight.

SETTING LIFESTYLE & HEALTH GOALS

You achieve success in life by focusing on and dedicating yourself to a goal. A goal gives you something to work towards. It helps you create a plan, a road map, to achieving what you want. So, where do you want to go? There's no point setting out on a journey if you have no idea where you want to end up. Think about what you want in your life, what you want to change and what you want to be like, physically and mentally. Then follow the steps below and start achieving your goals.

DECIDE ON YOUR LONG-TERM GOAL

Dedicate some time to decide on your long-term goal. Is it to lose a certain amount of weight? To lower your blood pressure to a certain point? To improve your overall wellbeing? To be able to run 5 kilometres? To be able to keep up with your kids? To fit into your wedding dress?

Once you have decided on your long-term goal, visualise it. What will it look like? What will it feel like? What will your life be like? The more feelings you can put into your goal, the more you will be committed to it and the more powerful it will be. The intensity of your feeling will strengthen your commitment to the goal and make it much more tangible. Your goal must be meaningful to you. How much do you really want to achieve this?

MAKE IT ACHIEVABLE AND REALISTIC

To effectively set a goal, it's important to be realistic in terms of what you want to achieve. You need to work with your body type and shape – don't subscribe to the unrealistic ideal body images often portrayed in the media. If you are 180 centimetres tall and currently weigh 120 kilograms, it's unrealistic to set a goal weight of 55 kilograms, whether it's in one year or five. Instead, pick a healthy weight for your height, a weight you feel you could live with, and then set in place the steps to achieve this goal.

To simply improve your health, your goal weight needs to be 5 to 10 per cent from your starting weight, or 6 to 12 kilograms if you weigh 120 kilograms now. If you choose an unrealistic or unachievable goal, you will have trouble committing to it and will most likely give up before you have made much progress. The danger is also that you will then give up forever.

If your goal is to improve your health by eating better but you know you can't live without chocolate, then be realistic and include some chocolate in your plan. For example, reduce your intake to one small snack-sized chocolate bar a day rather than a family-size block. If your goal includes giving up chocolate forever, you're unlikely to stick with it. Even with the best intentions, if you choose an unrealistic goal, deep down you won't really believe you can achieve it. This underlying doubt will undermine your efforts and you'll end up feeling like you can never succeed.

You must start by truly believing that you can achieve your goal.

MAKE IT SPECIFIC

Decide on the specific details of your goal. Think about what you want, how you're going to make it happen and when you are going to reach it. What will you need to achieve it – family support, time, gym membership? It's not enough to say 'exercise more' or 'eat well'. Say, 'To reach my end goal of losing 10 kilograms over six months, I will walk four times a week for 30 minutes and only have one take-away dinner and two nights of drinking alcohol a week'.

MAKE IT MEASURABLE AND TIMED

If your goal is 'I want to get fit', then it will be very hard to measure. What defines 'fit' to you? If it's being able to walk for an hour without stopping or lift a 20-kilogram weight or run 5 kilometres or swim 20 laps, then make this your goal. You want a goal with results you can see and measure. How else will you know what you're achieving? Include a timeframe. When do you want to achieve your goal by? What will your milestone dates be along the way?

BREAK YOUR LONG-TERM GOAL INTO MINI-GOALS

Setting short- and medium-term goals not only helps divide the main goal into bite-sized steps, but it also makes you more accountable for your actions and, most importantly, gives you a sense of success and achievement on the way to reaching your main goal. Without such steps, plans remain just that – plans that will never be fulfilled because there is no structure to make them happen. Give each step a suitable timeframe so that you can both achieve and measure your success. If your long-term goal is to lose 20 kilograms but your mini-goals are to lose 1 kilogram every two weeks, then every two weeks you'll know whether you're on track. Achieving your mini-goals will develop your strength of mind, boost your confidence and keep you motivated. They also give you a chance to reward yourself along the way.

You can even use small goals each day – apply them to your exercise workouts and eating plans so that you are focused on achieving specific outcomes.

ADD A REWARD

Remember to acknowledge your achievements on your way to your long-term goal. Reward yourself for each mini-goal you reach, be it losing 3 kilograms, running for 10 minutes without stopping or not drinking alcohol for a week. Choose life-affirming rewards. Now is the time to stop rewarding yourself with food and alcohol. Reward yourself with something meaningful to you, whether it's a new CD, a trip to the movies (no choc-top included), time with a friend, a long, hot bath or just some quiet time to yourself away from the family. Rewards keep you motivated. Decide ahead of time what your rewards will be for your mini-goals and your long-term goal, and write them down. Planning your rewards ahead of time will give you something to look forward to, keep you focused and help you create a new healthy habit of not using food as a reward.

WRITE DOWN YOUR GOALS

You have to 'own' your goals. If you really want to stay motivated, ensure you are losing weight for yourself and no one else, and that your goals are on your timeframe and no one else's. Write down all the reasons why you want to lose weight. This is the stage to focus on the future and think about what you want and how to make that happen, rather than dwell on the past and the reasons why you are where you are in the first place. What would it be like if your problem was solved? What will you notice, what will be different, how will you feel? Move towards your ideal future.

You may want to keep your goals to yourself or you may want to share them. Telling your friends, family and colleagues can be a positive step – not only for their support but also, by speaking your intent, you are reinforcing your decision to make positive change and are more likely to stick to your plans. Regularly reread your goals to see your progress. Remember that goals are flexible and you can adapt them at any stage to reflect changes in your life or in your priorities.

HOW TO EAT WELL

Before any attempt can be made to lose weight, you need to understand the basics of eating well. Once you know the right foods to eat and the right portion size, you're well on your way to good health and weight loss. To eat healthily you need some targets to guide your selection of foods. The easiest way to do this is to group similar foods together and then suggest a target number of serves per day, depending on your age and gender. The basic or staple food groups are vegetables (which includes salad), fruit, grains (which includes breads and cereals), dairy products, meat and meat alternatives (which includes lean red meat, chicken and other poultry, fish, soy beans and other beans, chickpeas, lentils, tofu, eggs and nuts) and, finally, healthy fats and oils.

THE SIX CORE FOOD GROUPS

1. Grains
2. Vegetables (including salad)
3. Fruit
4. Dairy products
5. Meat and meat alternatives
6. Fats and oils

1 GRAINS

Wholegrain or wholemeal breads and cereals are nutritious and filling. If you are not used to having wholemeal and wholegrain breads and cereals, start by switching to white high-fibre versions. You can gradually increase the proportion of grains that are wholemeal or wholegrain so your palate can adjust to the change and eventually switch to completely wholemeal and wholegrain products.

2 VEGETABLES (INCLUDING SALAD)

A variety of types and colours of vegetables will help you meet your vitamin, mineral and fibre needs. Vegetables and salad are high in nutrients and fibre, but low in kilojoules. Filling up on vegetables and salad will help you manage your hunger. Try new vegetables alongside the ones you like and gradually increase the amount and the variety.

3 FRUIT

Fruit is packed with fibre and nutrients, and is the perfect snack to have on the run. Take care not to go overboard with fruit and note that fruit juice is not the same as fresh fruit. One glass of fruit juice can contain the same kilojoules as two to three pieces of fresh fruit, yet you drink it in a flash compared to eating whole fruit.

4 DAIRY PRODUCTS

Dairy products are the richest source of calcium for building strong bones and teeth. Include reduced-fat dairy foods every day. If you do not eat dairy foods, you will need to include a calcium-fortified dairy alternative such as soy or rice milk.

5 MEAT AND MEAT ALTERNATIVES

Aim for the leanest meats you can afford. Regularly include the vegetarian choices or opt for meals that include meats alongside beans and lentils. Note that this saves you money in addition to being a healthier option.

6 FATS AND OILS

You only need small amounts of fats and oils to stay healthy. So use them sparingly on bread, toast or in cooking. Select the healthy versions, such as polyunsaturated and monounsaturated oils and margarine.

What's missing?

Foods and drinks not listed in the table are called the 'sometimes' or 'extras' group. This includes all those items that provide a lot of kilojoules, but a very limited amount of essential nutrients, such as vitamins, minerals and fibre. Extras include lollies, take-aways, soft drink, cordial, hot chips, biscuits and cakes and pastries. Ideally you would only have these items less than once a month.

GETTING THE BASICS RIGHT

Good nutrition relies on getting the basics right. You need to consistently consume a healthy diet that meets all your vitamin and mineral requirements. To consume a nutritionally adequate diet, include a wide variety of breads and cereals, fruit and vegetables, and dairy and meat products or alternatives on a daily basis. This can be done by choosing foods from each of the six food groups to help meet requirements for vitamins, minerals, carbohydrates, protein, fat and fibre. (Read the section 'What are the important nutrients?' on pages 16–19 for more about the essential nutrients.)

WHAT NOW?

Use the chart on the opposite page to guide your food choices. It outlines how much of each type of food you should be consuming to stay healthy and lose weight.

FOOD GROUP	SERVING SIZE	NUMBER OF SERVES EACH DAY	
		Women	Men
Vegetables	▪ 1/2 cup cooked vegetables ▪ 1 cup salad ▪ 1 medium potato	4-5+	5+
Fruit	▪ 1 medium piece of fresh fruit (e.g. apple or pear) ▪ 2 pieces small fruit (e.g. apricots or plums) ▪ 1 cup canned fruit or diced fruit ▪ 1 1/2 tablespoons dried fruit or a 30 g packet	2-3	2-4
Breads and cereals	▪ 1 slice of bread ▪ 1/2 medium bread roll ▪ 1/2 cup cooked rice, pasta or noodles ▪ 1/2 cup porridge ▪ 3/4 cup breakfast cereal flakes ▪ 2 Weet-Bix	4-5+	6+
Dairy products	▪ 1 cup (250 mL) milk ▪ 40 g (2 slices) cheese ▪ 200 g tub yoghurt ▪ 1 cup custard	2-3	2-4
Lean red meat, chicken and other poultry, fish, soy or other beans, chickpeas, lentils, tofu, eggs and nuts	▪ 65-100 g cooked lean meat or chicken ▪ 1/2 cup lean mince ▪ 2 small chops ▪ 2 slices roast meat ▪ 80-120 g cooked fish ▪ 2 small eggs ▪ 1/2 cup cooked soy, kidney, baked, canned or other beans, lentils, chickpeas or split peas ▪ 1/3 cup nuts ▪ 2 tablespoons peanut butter	1-1 1/2	1-2
Healthy fats and oils	▪ 1 teaspoon polyunsaturated or monounsaturated oil or margarine	2-3	2-4

WHAT ARE THE IMPORTANT NUTRIENTS?

When it comes to establishing good patterns of health, we have to remember that we can't simply cut out food without being aware of the important nutrients. Food contains lots of important nutrients. These are divided into macro (big) nutrients, with protein, fats and carbohydrates being the main ones, and micro (small) nutrients, which include vitamins, minerals and phytonutrients. This section explains what these nutrients are and which foods contain them and then sets out some foundations for creating the right set-up at home to keep you healthy.

If you were building a house, then the macronutrients would be equivalent to building materials like bricks, wood, steel, insulation, plumbing and roofing. The micronutrients are just as important as the macro ones and include the nails, screws, wire, adhesives and plaster. Leave these out and you could still build a house, but it would not pass a building inspection and would be unlikely to stand up to rough weather. You need to get the right amount of nutrients from your foods every day.

CARBOHYDRATES AND FIBRE

Carbohydrates (often called 'carbs') are used in your body as fuel and are the fuel your body runs on best, just like petrol in a car. If you don't eat enough carbohydrates, your body will obtain energy from less optimal sources. And, if you choose the right type of carbohydrates, you'll also ensure you are getting enough dietary fibre.

Fibre is just a very complex form of carbohydrate and helps to reduce the risk of you becoming constipated or developing diverticulitis or eventually colon cancer. Fibre is only found in plant foods. It cannot be digested by the body and therefore passes fairly quickly through the digestive tract, collecting waste as it goes. Dietary fibre is a key factor in controlling your appetite and, because it needs more chewing, it helps you feel more satisfied after eating (so you eat less).

During weight loss, maintaining a high-fibre intake of around 30 grams per day and drinking up to 2 litres of fluids can help to reduce your risk of gallstones. It is best to increase your fibre intake through food. Choose high-fibre carbohydrates, such as wholemeal and wholegrain bread, pasta and breakfast cereal; psyllium husks; wheat bran or oat bran; brown rice; chickpeas; lentils; soy beans; baked beans and red kidney beans. Eating these high-fibre foods combined with two serves of fruit and five serves of vegetables or salad will ensure you are getting enough fibre to maintain good health.

However, if you need a supplement, choose one that is low in or free of sugar. Take it between meals and away from any medications (its binding effect may reduce their efficacy). Increase your water intake and start with a small fibre dose, then gradually increase it.

PROTEIN

Protein is the main structural nutrient and is used to make and repair all cells throughout the body, including the organs, such as the heart and kidneys, as well as muscle, hair and nails. Enzymes that control the major metabolic processes are also made from very specific proteins. Protein is made from building blocks called amino acids and there are a number of essential amino acids that need to be consumed from foods like meat, fish, chicken, dairy products, legumes, nuts and seeds. Enzymes work a lot like a set of traffic lights, directing the metabolic processes that govern digestion, respiration, infection and immunity.

During weight loss, having enough protein helps to protect muscles, but you only need approximately 0.8 to 1 gram of protein per kilogram of body weight per day.

GOOD FATS

All fat is high in kilojoules which can quickly add up and undo our weight loss efforts if we are not careful. However, our bodies need some fat. Fat contains fatty acids and many of these are essential for building healthy cell membranes that then protect every cell in your body. Fat also regulates body processes such as blood clotting and immune function, and the type of fat in food influences processes such as inflammation. All bodies need some fat stores in order to provide a layer of insulation and protection for the vital organs. Fat also allows a back-up supply of the fat-soluble vitamins A, D, E and K to be stored.

During weight loss, consuming no fat at all can increase your risk of gallstones. To reduce your risk of gallstones you need to eat at least 20 grams of healthy fats from your foods each day. Healthy fats include sunflower, safflower, canola or olive oils and margarines made from these, plus nuts, seeds, avocado and fish oils.

Unhealthy fats should be avoided; these include saturated and trans-fats. Saturated fat raises cholesterol in your body and is found in animal products such as meat, full-fat dairy products and butter as well as coconut oil and palm oil. Most take-away foods, biscuits, cakes and pastries are also high in saturated fat. Trans-fats are created when some margarines, shortenings and solid spreads used in the food industry are made. In your body they act like saturated fats. Even though Australian spreads contain much lower levels of trans-fats than those in the USA they are best avoided by selecting low trans-fat margarines and avoiding processed foods, especially those high in fat such as pastries, biscuits and deep-fried foods.

VITAMIN	GOOD FOOD SOURCES	FUNCTION IN THE BODY
Thiamin (Vitamin B1)	Wholemeal breads and cereals, wheat germ, wheat bran, sesame seeds, soy beans and other dried beans and peas, fortified breakfast cereals, Vegemite and Promite, watermelon, yeast and pork.	To metabolise carbohydrate and convert glucose into energy. Used in nerves, and to maintain muscles.
Riboflavin (Vitamin B2)	Milk, yoghurt, cheese, wholegrain breads and cereals, egg whites, leafy green vegetables, mushrooms, Vegemite and Promite, meat, liver and kidney.	To release energy from food and support healthy eyes and skin.
Vitamin B3 (niacin)	Lean meat, milk, eggs, wholegrain breads and cereals, tuna, salmon, nuts, leafy green vegetables.	To metabolise protein, fat, carbohydrate and alcohol which produces energy. Helps to lower cholesterol, maintain healthy skin, nerves and digestive system.
Folic acid (folate)	Green leafy vegetables, legumes, seeds, liver, poultry, eggs, cereals and citrus fruits. Many cereal-based foods in Australia, such as bread and breakfast cereals, are fortified with folate.	To form red blood cells, which carry oxygen around the body. Helps development of a healthy baby in pregnant women. Used in DNA synthesis and cell growth. Women of child-bearing age or planning a pregnancy need a diet rich in folic acid and should consider taking supplements or eat fortified foods to reduce the risk of neural tube defects such as spina bifida in the baby.
Vitamin C	Fruit, especially citrus, pineapple, mango and pawpaw. Vegetables, especially capsicum, broccoli, brussels sprouts, cabbage, spinach.	To help with iron absorption and in wound healing and fighting infection. Used in making connective tissue and blood vessels for healthy teeth, gums and bones.
Beta-carotene (Vitamin A precursor)	Dark yellow and orange and dark green vegetables and fruit such as apricots, mango and rockmelon, carrots, sweet potato and pumpkin, spinach and broccoli.	Beta-carotene is converted to retinol in the intestine. Retinol is used to convert light to images sent to your brain as sight. Needed for normal growth, to help fight infections and can act as an antioxidant.
Vitamin D	Formed in the skin from sunlight. Oily fish, eggs, margarine, butter, cheese and fish oils.	Promotes strong bone development and helps with the absorption of calcium and phosphorus.

MINERAL	GOOD FOOD SOURCES	FUNCTION IN THE BODY
Zinc	Meat, chicken, fish, oysters, legumes, nuts, wholemeal and wholegrain products.	To help in wound healing, development of the immune system and other functions.
Iron	There are two types of iron: **haem iron**, found in animal foods such as beef and fish; and **non-haem iron**, found in plant foods such as beans, nuts and leafy greens.	To make haemoglobin in red blood cells and prevent anaemia. Assists enzymes needed in chemical reactions in the body. Vitamin C, meat and cooking boost iron absorption.
Calcium	Dairy foods, canned salmon and sardines with bones, fortified soy milks, leafy green vegetables, brazil nuts, almonds and sesame seed paste (tahini).	To make bones and teeth. For healthy nerves, regulating muscle contraction and relaxation, regulating heart function, blood clotting, nerve transmission and enzyme function.
Magnesium	Tofu, soy beans, nuts, seeds, lean meat, spinach, barley, wheatgerm, brown rice, avocado, bananas, peanut butter and peas.	To make new cells and for healthy heart and muscle contraction. Needed for enzymes that release energy in the body.

NUTRIENT	GOOD FOOD SOURCES	FUNCTION IN THE BODY
Protein	Meat, fish, chicken, dairy products, legumes, nuts, eggs and seeds.	Made from building blocks, called amino acids, that are used to make and repair all cells in the body.
Fat	Sunflower, safflower, canola or olive oils or margarines, nuts or seeds and avocado. Saturated fat comes from animal products such as meat and full-fat dairy products.	Body fat insulates and protects the vital organs, carries and stores the fat-soluble vitamins. Used in all cell membranes and to make chemicals essential to regulate body processes such as inflammation, blood clotting and immune function.
Carbohydrate	Wholemeal and wholegrain bread and pasta products, cereal, brown rice, low-fat dairy products, fruit and vegetables, salad, legumes such as chickpeas and lentils.	The preferred source of fuel for the body. Helps to conserve protein for the body.
Fibre	Vegetables, salad, fruit, wholemeal and wholegrain bread and cereals, chickpeas, lentils, soy beans, baked beans, red kidney beans, psyllium husks, wheat bran or oat bran added to breakfast cereal.	A high-fibre diet helps to reduce the risk of constipation and gallstones in the short term and diverticulitis and colon cancer in the long term.

INTERPRETING FOOD LABELS

Every food product in the supermarket must have a nutrition label on it. This label is called a Nutrition Information Panel or NIP. Food Standards Australia and New Zealand (FSANZ) have legislated that food products must display an NIP. The only exceptions are fruit and vegetables; very small packages the size of a chewing gum packet; foods that have no significant nutritional value, such as a single herb or spice, tea, and coffee; foods sold unpackaged; and foods that are made and packaged at the point of sale, such as bread from a local bakery.

You can use food labels to help you choose foods that are a healthy addition to your supermarket trolley, as well as to identify nasty products that you ought to leave on the supermarket shelf.

The first useful piece of information to locate on the label is the ingredient list. The ingredients are listed on food labels in their descending order of weight. This means that the ingredient that is listed first is present in the greatest amount and the ingredient listed second is present in the second greatest amount, and so on.

Products must also report the percentages of key ingredients. For example, mango yoghurt must state the percentage (%) of mango in the product, then all of the other ingredients must be listed.

Sometimes the words used to describe the ingredients can be complicated and confusing. There can be different types of a similar ingredient in the food. For instance, did you know that all these words mean sugar: sucrose, fructose, corn syrup solids and cane sugar?

It makes sense to choose products that contain ingredients that you recognise; this way, you are more likely to pick the products that are less processed and closer to nature than others.

THESE WORDS MEAN ...

Fat: vegetable oil, animal fat, copha, coconut oil, palm oil, shortening, margarine, butter, lard, beef fat, creamed, toasted, milk solids, oven fried/baked, dripping, monoglycerides, diglycerides, cream, mayonnaise, sour cream

Sugar: raw sugar, brown sugar, honey, corn syrup, malt, golden syrup, glucose, disaccharides, monosaccharides, fructose, sucrose, lactose, maltose, dextrose, molasses, mannitol, sorbitol, xylitol

FOOD LABEL CLAIMS

Labels can contain claims about the products with a range of words used that can confuse and distract you when it comes to choosing exactly which food product to add to your trolley. The chart on the opposite page outlines some that you are likely to come across.

COMMON CLAIMS ON FOOD LABELS	
Low in fat	Contains 3 grams of fat or less per 100 grams of product.
Reduced fat	Contains at least 25 per cent less fat than the usual version of this food.
High fibre	Contains at least 3 grams of fibre per serve.
Very high fibre	Contains at least 6 grams of fibre per serve.
Low sugar	Contains 15 grams sugar or less per 100 grams of product.
No added sugar	Does not contain added sugar, but may contain 'natural' sugars that come from fruit and milk. These foods are not necessarily lower in kilojoules than other foods.
Low-calorie	Contains almost no kilojoules or calories.
Diet	Usually means the product is artificially sweetened and has a lower kilojoule count compared to regular versions.
95% fat-free	This product has 5 per cent fat, or 5 grams of fat per 100 grams of product. As a comparison, 1 teaspoon of margarine contains about 4 grams of fat.
Pick the tick	Foods with the Heart Foundation 'tick' have met strict guidelines for being reduced or low in saturated fat, salt and kilojoules and may also be higher in fibre, depending on the category. The 'tick' is a useful guide for making healthy choices. Not all foods apply to undergo the strict accreditation process to earn the 'tick'. However, you can use the nutrition information panels from these products to compare with labels on similar products.
Light/Lite	This can refer to the colour, flavour, texture or the salt or fat content of food. The product may not be a healthy choice, or low in kilojoules at all.
Cholesterol-free	This can be misleading. These foods can still be high in fat, for example peanut butter, olive oil and avocados, and therefore high in kilojoules. All vegetable and plant foods are cholesterol-free because pre-formed cholesterol is only found in animal products. Our bodies make cholesterol from saturated fat so avoiding products high in saturated fat is always important when making food choices.
All natural	This is not a guarantee that this product is good for you. Sugar, oil, butter and cream are all natural ingredients.
Saturated, monounsaturated and polyunsaturated fats	Saturated fat, mainly found in animal foods, is the major fat that increases blood cholesterol levels. All types of fats have the same number of calories but mono and poly fats are important in small amounts to keep your heart healthy. In excess, they still lead to weight gain. All fats provide 37 kilojoules or 10 calories per gram. This compares to carbohydrates and protein, which are both 4 calories per gram.
Trans-fat	These occur in small amounts naturally in dairy products, beef and lamb but most trans-fat comes from solid margarines and cooking fats used in processed foods, such as pies, pastries, cakes, biscuits, buns and in some margarines.

PLANNING YOUR MEALS

To be successful in losing weight and keeping it off for good, you need to plan your meals and snacks ahead of time. Plan them out a whole week in advance. Next, write out a matching grocery list. Do your grocery shopping straight after breakfast or lunch because you make more impulse buys if you are hungry. Do not buy foods that are not on your grocery list or foods that you know should not be in your pantry, refrigerator or freezer. Compare food labels to make sure you get the healthiest version of products. At home, modify your favorite recipes to ensure they are lower in saturated fat and kilojoules and serve meals with a generous amount of salad and/or vegetables.

AVOIDING TEMPTATION

Too tempted? Planning ahead saves you from having to rely on willpower. Keeping an apple and some sugar-free chewing gum in your handbag, your work bag, car or desk drawer means you always have an easy alternative to the temptations that surround you at every turn.

DEALING WITH BAD DAYS

If you have a bad day, the first step is to give up the guilt. Do not beat yourself up about it - you're human after all. There will always be temptations and obstacles in your way, so turn them into positives. Learn from any lapse you may have had. How did it make you feel? What behaviour will you choose in the future to avoid the same thing happening again? Decide how to deal with your triggers, whatever they may be. Start dealing with things directly and find coping strategies that are right for you.

Take it day by day. If you have a bad day (or week, or month) and end up eating too much, or bingeing, or not exercising, do not give up. One day does not mean there's no point for the rest of your life. It's so easy to give up but you get nothing and will never, ever be the person you want to be. It's easy to fall back into old bad habits, especially when food provides comfort, but these habits are self-destructive. You can't build a new habit - or change your life - in a day. It takes time, patience and commitment to learn new skills.

If it works for you, follow the 80/20 rule: if you stay on the path to your goal 80 per cent of the time, giving yourself 20 per cent as room to move, you'll stay committed and still achieve your goal. It may take a little longer but it keeps you on track and it's realistic.

Stop thinking 'all or nothing' or 'good and bad'. Make a resolve right now that you will not give up on your new healthy lifestyle, even if you have a lapse for a moment, day or week. Choose not to be discouraged or feel guilty about this; no one is perfect and sometimes you have to miss a workout or you do indulge. Just be confident in yourself that you will resume your healthy eating and exercise plans. And do something as soon as possible that gets you back on track, such as going for a walk or making your next meal extra healthy.

HEALTHY EATING TIPS

1 Eat breakfast every day. Breakfast eaters have been shown to have more willpower in the mornings. If you think you are too busy for breakfast, set the table the night before and put the alarm on for 5 minutes earlier, or pack your breakfast in a lunchbox and take it to work.

2 If snacking is your biggest temptation, plan to have a favourite snack every day and work it into your kilojoule count. Pack your snacks for the day ahead into your lunchbox.

3 At dinner, use smaller-sized plates, cups and bowls so your eyes and brain think you have eaten more than you really have.

4 If fast food restaurants are a magnet for you, then you may need to plan your driving routes ahead of time so that you do not drive past them.

5 At coffee shops, never pick up the menu. Order a coffee without even looking at the menu to avoid that 'just this once' temptation.

6 Do not buy anything that is sold in multi-bags. Multi-anything means multi-tempting.

7 Only purchase foods that fit with your healthy eating plan and that you really want to eat.

8 Plan all meals ahead so you are not tempted to give in to take-aways.

9 Get your fruit and vegetables home-delivered so you feel you have to use them up.

10 Never, never, never go to an all-you-can-eat buffet, for very obvious reasons.

11 Never eat in front of the television because it creates eating amnesia and you have no idea what you have eaten. If you do watch television, get up in the ad breaks, because food advertising works and it will tempt you to buy and eat more of the wrong stuff.

12 Swap whole milk and full-fat yoghurt and cheese to reduced-fat or skim varieties.

13 Swap sweetened beverages to water or reduced-fat or skim milk.

14 Serve potato without fat, which means swap hot chips and fries to mashed, boiled or homemade chips without using fat.

15 Buy the leanest meat you can afford and trim off all visible fat.

16 Use low-fat cooking techniques (see Cooking Basics for more information about low-fat cooking techniques).

17 Swap high-fat cereal-based foods and snacks, such as the ones that come in multi-bags, biscuits, cakes, pastries and crisps to lower fat choices like raisin bread, low-fat yoghurt, fruit, air-popped popcorn or packaged snacks containing fewer than 400 kilojoules per serve.

18 Limit 'extras' to an agreed number per week and when that limit is reached, there are no more until next week.

COOKING BASICS

One of the keys for losing weight is to take control of your food consumption. One of the best ways to be in control is to select and cook your own food. You will have much more control over your diet if you know exactly what has been bought rather than relying on highly processed or take-away foods. There are a few things to keep in mind before cooking food, one of which is the safe selection of foods.

Selecting and keeping food safe

In Australia, our love of eating outdoors, the hot weather, and our use of convenience foods increases the risk of food poisoning. The food-safety tips provided here will help you keep your food safe. This issue is so important that in the Biggest Loser House, contestants are taken through this guide when they first arrive.

WHAT ARE 'BEST-BEFORE' AND 'USE-BY' DATES?

- Foods must have a 'best-before' date stamped on the package if they have a shelf-life of less than 2 years. After this date they will start to lose quality and nutritional value, but they may still be safe to eat.
- If correctly stored at the supermarket and at home these foods will stay fresh and of good quality, right up until the 'best-before' date. These foods may need to be kept at specific temperatures in the fridge or freezer to maintain their quality.
- Frozen and canned products usually maintain their quality for a reasonable length of time after the 'best-before' date. However, extra care needs to be taken with any chilled products. Select these just before you head to the supermarket checkout and store them in an esky in the car as they could spoil before the 'best-before' date if not kept cold enough. Put these items away as soon as you get home.
- A 'use-by' date means that foods should not be consumed after this date. An exception is bread with a shelf-life of less than 7 days, which can instead have a 'baked-on' or 'baked-for' date.
- Always check the food packaging to make sure it is not damaged and that products have been stored appropriately before you purchase them.

HOW DO YOU KEEP FOOD SAFE?

The most common reason food poisoning occurs is that food has not been cooked for long enough or at a high enough temperature to kill bacteria. Some foods naturally carry more bacteria on them than others and so extra care needs to be taken to make sure they are cooked thoroughly and handled carefully. These foods include meat, poultry, eggs, dairy products, processed meats, such as salami and ham, seafood, cooked rice and pasta, and pre-prepared salads.

For meat, most food-poisoning bacteria are on the outer surface, so it's important never to return cooked meat to a tray that had raw meat on it or you risk transferring bacteria from the tray to the cooked meat.

The danger zone for food poisoning is in the temperature zone between the range of 5 degrees Celsius and 70 degrees Celsius. The shorter the time food spends in this zone, the lower the risk of food poisoning. There are some easy food practices to follow to minimise the time food spends in the danger zone. Serve cold food straight from the fridge. Hot food should be hot enough that you can see steam rising from it. Once cooked, foods should be eaten promptly. If they can't be, then keep them hot; otherwise cool them until the steam stops rising, then cover them and store in the fridge or freezer. Hot food will cool faster if you put it into shallow containers or divide it into smaller portions first.

You can keep cooked foods in the fridge for up to a few days, but if you want to keep it longer than this then put it into the freezer as soon as it has cooled.

In the fridge, take care to ensure cooked foods are kept on the top shelves and anything raw is stored on the bottom shelves to avoid any condensation from raw food falling on cooked food and contaminating it. When defrosting foods, place them in the fridge to keep them below 5 degrees Celsius and out of the food danger zone. Never leave it on a benchtop at room temperature because this is the food poisoning temperature zone.

When food is re-heated, it needs to be steaming hot. If you are using a microwave to cook or reheat foods, then stop the microwave and stir foods periodically during cooking to ensure all parts are adequately cooked or re-heated. Cut foods into even-sized pieces and ensure lids fit well so the steam stays trapped in the dish and helps the foods to cook well. Let the foods stand for the recommended time after the microwave stops because they keep cooking due to the trapped steam. If food gets left out and has been in the temperature danger zone, then throw it out rather than risk food poisoning.

When eating outdoors, take care to make sure foods do not get contaminated from insects, pests and animals by keeping them covered. When cooking on a barbecue, transfer cooked items to a clean plate and never re-use the same plate or container that held raw foods. Minimise the time foods spend in the danger temperature zone by leaving meats in the fridge until you are ready to cook them and, once cooked, keeping them warm or serving. Keep salads cool by leaving them in the fridge or cool esky until ready to serve. Then, as soon as people are finished serving themselves, cover and return to the fridge or esky as soon as is practical. Some people have a lower level of immunity to food poisoning bacteria and are at greater risk than others. This includes young children, pregnant women, the elderly and anyone with a chronic illness. This means extra care must be taken with their food preparation. Never give people in this group raw egg because it can harbour large amounts of bacteria and needs to be cooked thoroughly.

GETTING READY TO COOK

Make it easier to cook healthy meals by ensuring you have healthy basics in your kitchen. This means that you will be less tempted to call for home delivery or to get take-away because you will be able to whip up a tasty healthy treat faster than the delivery driver can get to your place.

Have three easy meals that you can prepare in under 20 minutes and permanently add their ingredients to your weekly shopping list.

HEALTHY COOKING

Healthy eating is delicious when you know some of the tricks of the trade. By changing an ingredient or cooking technique, you can update recipes and create healthy versions of your favourite foods.

RECIPE MAKEOVERS

- Give recipes a weight-loss makeover by swapping unhealthy ingredients for healthy ingredients, reducing their amounts or even removing them.
- Swap high-fat cooking techniques for low-fat cooking methods.
- Use herbs and spices to add flavour without adding fat or kilojoules.

FLAVOUR WITHOUT FAT

- Add stewed fruit or a chopped banana to cereal.
- Grate an apple into rolled oats before cooking.
- Top toast with cooked mushrooms, tomatoes, capsicum or sweet corn.
- Heat chopped leftover vegetables and serve as a topping for toast; add an egg or reduced-fat cheese to make a meal.

HEALTHY SNACKS

- Cut up fruit for a fruit platter.
- Pack fresh fruit into your lunchbox.
- Top English muffins or crumpets with tomato paste, diced vegetables and sprinkle with reduced-fat cheese for a quick mini pizza.
- Serve carrot and celery sticks, florets of broccoli and cauliflower and strips of capsicum with a low-fat dip.
- Grate or dice onion, carrot, zucchini, potato and corn into a savoury muffin or into pikelet mixture.

MAIN MEALS

- Make meat go further by adding extra vegetables to a stir-fry or a casserole.
- Add extra vegetables, dried peas, beans or lentils to recipes for meatloaf, patties, stuffings, soups, stews and casseroles, pies, nachos, pasta and rice dishes, pizzas and pancakes.
- Serve main meals with cooked vegetables and a salad of baby spinach leaves and cherry tomatoes and olives.
- Use capsicum, zucchini, pumpkin, eggplant, cabbage and lettuce leaves as edible containers and fill with savoury toppings.
- For easy and healthy wedges, cut potato, sweet potato, pumpkin and parsnip into wedges; microwave until cooked; mix with a teaspoon of vegetable oil, dried mixed herbs and Cajun seasoning and bake in a hot oven until crispy.

HOW HERBS AND SPICES CAN HELP

When you cook without fat you risk losing some of the taste because many flavour components are absorbed by fat. Herbs and spices are the answer: they can enhance the taste of any dish and the bonus is that they will lower the amount of sodium in any meal because you won't need to use any salt.

When cooking with fresh herbs, add them close to the end of the cooking time as they lose their flavour with prolonged cooking. If you have fresh herbs left over, you can either purée them with lemon or lime juice and store in the fridge or chop, mix with water and freeze in ice cube trays to keep for adding to cooked dishes.

When using dried herbs you need to use about one-quarter of the amount compared to a fresh herb. This does vary and you will need to experiment to find out what is right for your taste buds.

EASY IDEAS TO REDUCE FAT AND KILOJOULES IN RECIPES	
Milk, yoghurt, cream and sour cream	■ Use skim or low-fat varieties of dairy products. ■ Replace cream with skim plain yoghurt or a can of evaporated skim milk. ■ Replace sour cream with skim plain yoghurt mixed with a teaspoon of lemon juice or vinegar.
Cheese	■ Use 50% reduced-fat cheese and use smaller amounts than the recipe suggest. ■ Try cottage cheese or ricotta cheese on sandwiches. ■ Use an extra-light cheese slice to thicken sauces. ■ Mix grated reduced-fat cheese with grated carrot for tacos or sandwich fillings. ■ Mix grated reduced-fat cheese with breadcrumbs or oats for pie toppings.
Butter	■ Use reduced-fat margarine spreads for sandwiches. ■ In cooking, swap butter, lard, copha or cooking fats for polyunsaturated or monounsaturated margarine. ■ Cut the amount of margarine in recipes by about one-quarter and replace with apple purée.
Oil	■ Use a cooking oil spray to stir-fry. ■ Reduce the amount of oils in recipes, and use oils such as canola or sunflower.
Mayonnaise and salad dressing	■ Select fat-free varieties of mayonnaise and salad dressing. ■ Make your own salad dressing using ingredients such as low-fat yoghurt, buttermilk, tomato paste, balsamic or other vinegars, lemon juice, ricotta cheese, mustard and fruit pulp.
Sauces	■ Dilute creamy sauces with evaporated skim milk. ■ Dilute pasta or tomato-based sauces with canned tomato purée.
Meat and poultry	■ Remove the skin from poultry before cooking. ■ Choose lean meats and remove all visible fat. ■ Simmer mince for bolognese, cool and then skim the fat from the surface. ■ Bulk up casseroles with vegetables, canned tomatoes or legumes, such as canned kidney beans, chickpeas or brown lentils. ■ Cook stews the day before you need them. The fat can then be scraped off the top.
Pastry	■ Rather than shortcrust pastry, use filo pastry, spraying every three layers with an oil spray. ■ For a quick quiche crust, cover the base of a pie plate with rolled oats and rub ½ cup reduced-fat grated cheese through it.
Coconut cream or coconut milk	■ Use reduced-fat evaporated milk with a drop of coconut essence or use coconut-flavoured evaporated skim milk.

Desserts

Sweet treats can still be part of a healthy lifestyle – indulge without the guilt with these healthy and delicious recipes. Keep in mind that these desserts still need to be counted into your daily intake!

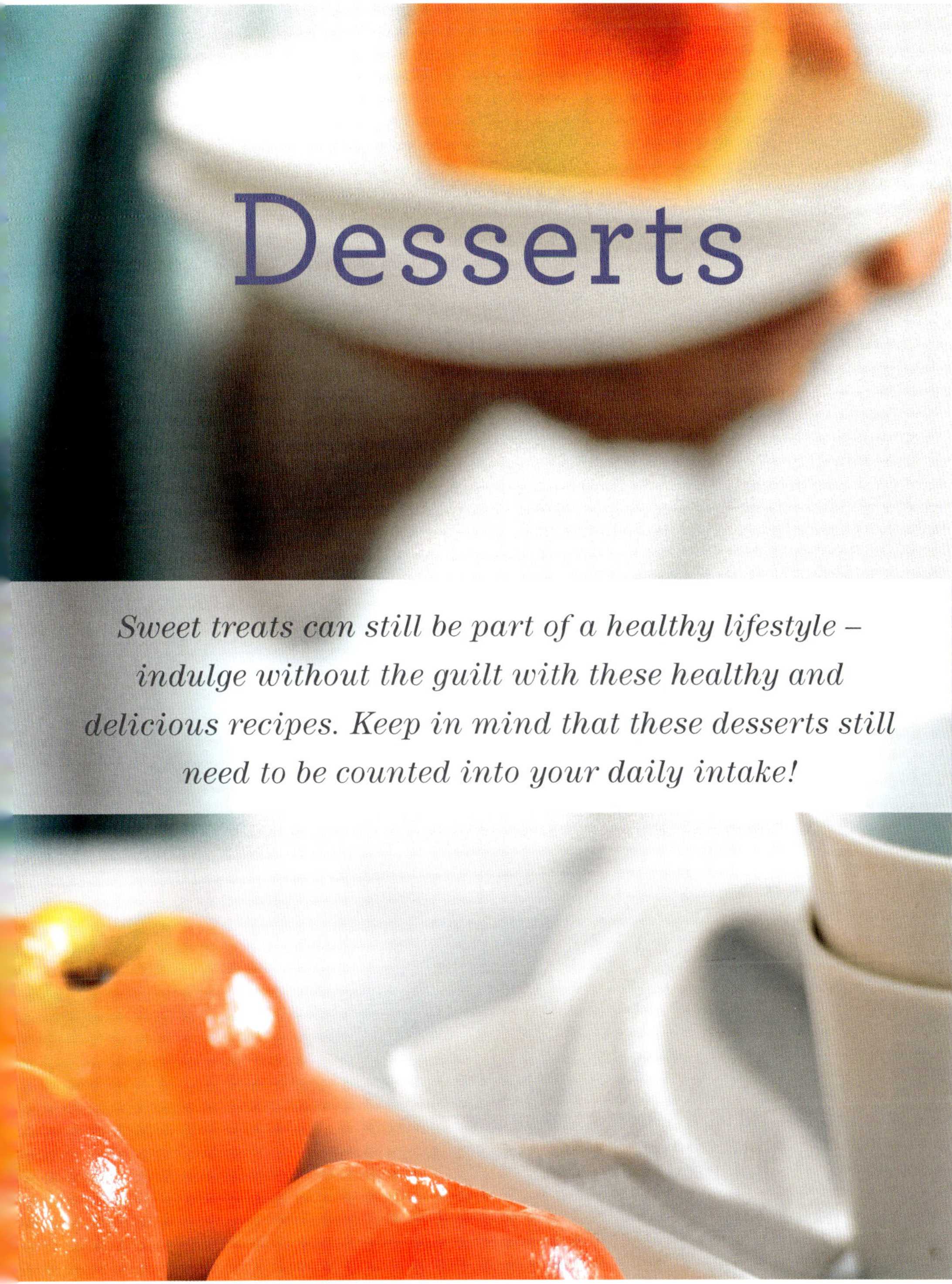

RASPBERRY & RICOTTA PARFAITS WITH ALMOND BREAD

A parfait is a classic dessert made from layering different ingredients. In this version, raspberry and ricotta are combined for a perfect low-fat treat.

SERVES 4 | PREPARATION 10 MINUTES | COOKING NIL

250 g fresh or thawed frozen raspberries, plus extra to garnish
2 tablespoons orange juice
2 teaspoons icing sugar, plus 2 teaspoons extra
250 g (1 cup) low-fat ricotta
½ teaspoon vanilla bean paste
2 tablespoons chopped toasted almonds
4 slices almond bread, to serve

Place the raspberries, orange juice and icing sugar in a bowl and stir to combine, then set aside to macerate for 5 minutes.

Meanwhile, place the ricotta, extra icing sugar, vanilla and almonds in a bowl and stir to combine.

To serve, place one-eighth of the raspberries in the base of four small serving glasses. Top each with a dollop of the ricotta mixture. Repeat with another layer of raspberries and finish with a dollop of ricotta and some raspberries on top.

Serve with a slice of almond bread on the side.

TIP *These parfaits are just as good with other berries – try strawberries, blueberries or blackberries or a mixture of all three.*

860 kj
Fat 12 g
Saturated fat 4 g
Carbohydrates 13 g
Protein 10.0 g
Sugars 10.5 g
Fibre 4.4 g

PER SERVE

APPLE & FRESH DATE CRUMBLE

We know that apple crumble is a family favourite, so we have made a low-fat version that everyone can enjoy.

SERVES 4 | PREPARATION 15 MINUTES | COOKING 15 MINUTES

4 Golden Delicious apples, peeled, cored and chopped
100 g fresh dates, pitted and chopped
80 ml (1/3 cup) fresh orange juice
1 cinnamon stick
1/3 cup rolled oats
1/3 cup slivered almonds
2 tablespoons shredded coconut
light cream, to serve (optional)

Preheat oven to 180°C or 160°C fan-forced. Place the apples, dates, orange juice and cinnamon stick in a saucepan and bring to the boil. Reduce the heat and simmer, covered, for 2–3 minutes or until the apples are just tender.

Discard the cinnamon stick and divide the mixture among four 125 ml (½ cup) ovenproof dishes. Combine the oats, almonds and coconut. Sprinkle over the top, then bake for 8–10 minutes. Serve with cream if desired.

940 kj
Fat 9.9 g
Saturated fat 1.6 g
Carbohydrates 27.5 g
Protein 4.7 g
Sugars 20.9 g
Fibre 5.6 g

PER SERVE

APPLES IN PASSIONFRUIT SYRUP

For a low-fat dessert idea, try these apples and passionfruit in warm syrup with a dollop of Greek-style yoghurt.

SERVES 4 | PREPARATION 10 MINUTES | COOKING 20 MINUTES

4 Granny Smith apples, peeled and cut into round slices 1 cm thick

4 passionfruit, halved

½ cup caster sugar

2 strips lemon rind

Greek-style yoghurt, to serve

Put the apples in a large saucepan with the passionfruit pulp, sugar, lemon rind and 125 ml (½ cup) water. Stir over medium heat until the sugar dissolves, then cover and bring to the boil.

Reduce the heat to low and simmer, uncovered, for 15 minutes or until tender. Serve warm or chilled with a dollop of yoghurt.

741 kj
Fat 1.2 g
Saturated fat 0.7 g
Carbohydrates 35.5 g
Protein 4.1 g
Sugars 34.8 g
Fibre 4.8 g

PER SERVE

RICOTTA BERRY CHEESECAKE

This crustless cheesecake is a great way to have your cake and eat it too!

SERVES 8 | PREPARATION 10 MINUTES | COOKING 50 MINUTES

- melted butter, to grease
- 1 cup smooth reduced-fat ricotta
- 100 g light cream cheese, at room temperature
- ⅓ cup caster sugar
- 2 eggwhites
- 1 egg
- 1 tablespoon finely grated lemon zest
- 1 tablespoon plain flour
- 35 g blueberries
- 250 g strawberries, halved
- icing sugar, to dust

504 kj
Fat 4.5 g
Saturated fat 2.6 g
Carbohydrates 12.5 g
Protein 7.4 g
Sugars 11.5 g
Fibre 0.9 g

PER SERVE

Preheat oven to 180°C or 160°C fan-forced. Lightly brush a 20 cm non-stick springform tin with melted butter.

Using electric beaters, beat the ricotta, cream cheese and sugar together until smooth. Add the eggwhites and egg, one at a time, beating well after each addition until combined. Stir in the lemon zest and flour. Pour half the mixture into the prepared tin and sprinkle with the blueberries. Pour in the remaining mixture and use the back of a spoon to smooth the surface.

Bake the cheesecake for 50 minutes or until golden brown and just firm to the touch. Turn off the oven and leave the cheesecake to cool, with the oven door slightly ajar, for 30 minutes.

Remove the cheesecake from the tin. Top with the strawberries and dust with icing sugar. Cut into wedges to serve.

APRICOT YOGHURT BRÛLÉES

Whip up this low-fat dessert in a flash.

SERVES 4 | PREPARATION 5 MINUTES | COOKING 5 MINUTES

825 g tin apricot halves in juice
1 cup low-fat natural yoghurt
2 tablespoons honey
¼ teaspoon ground cinnamon
½ cup caster sugar

Divide the apricot halves and a little of the juice among four 250-ml (1-cup) heatproof serving glasses.

Combine the yoghurt, honey and cinnamon in a small bowl. Spoon the yoghurt mixture over the apricots.

Place the sugar in a frying pan over low heat. Cook, stirring, for 3–5 minutes or until the sugar dissolves and caramelises. Remove the pan from the heat and set aside until the bubbles subside. Spoon the toffee over the yoghurt mixture and serve immediately.

1099 kj
Fat 0.1 g
Saturated fat 0.1 g
Carbohydrates 60.3 g
Protein 5.5 g
Sugars 57.4 g
Fibre 4.0 g

PER SERVE

DATE & CARROT PUDDINGS

Make sure you grease the ramekins well so that these delicious puddings don't stick.

SERVES 4 | PREPARATION 25 MINUTES | COOKING 25 MINUTES

½ cup fresh dates, pitted and chopped
½ teaspoon bicarbonate of soda
30 g low-fat dairy spread
2 tablespoons brown sugar
1 egg
1 teaspoon vanilla essence
½ small carrot, grated
½ cup self-raising flour
1 teaspoon pure icing sugar
150 g tub low-fat vanilla Frûche, to serve

Preheat oven to 190°C or 170°C fan-forced. Grease four 200-ml ramekins or pudding moulds. Line the bases with baking paper.

Combine the dates and 125 ml (½ cup) cold water in a small saucepan over medium–high heat. Bring to the boil, then reduce the heat to low and simmer for 2 minutes. Remove from the heat. Stir in the bicarbonate of soda, then set aside to cool.

Using an electric mixer, beat the dairy spread and brown sugar until well combined. Add the egg and vanilla essence and beat well. Stir in the carrot and the date mixture.

Sift the flour over the date mixture and stir gently to combine. Spoon into the prepared ramekins and place on a baking tray. Bake for 15–20 minutes or until a skewer inserted into the centre comes out clean. Stand for 5 minutes, then turn out onto serving plates. Dust with icing sugar and serve warm with Frûche.

889 kj
Fat 6.5 g
Saturated fat 2.7 g
Carbohydrates 33.4 g
Protein 4.7 g
Sugars 21.0 g
Fibre 2.3 g

PER SERVE

HONEY-GRILLED FIGS WITH VANILLA YOGHURT

A simple yet sophisticated dish – high in dietary fibre, the small luscious fig provides a sweet and satisfying dessert.

SERVES 4 | PREPARATION 5 MINUTES | COOKING 5 MINUTES

6 small ripe figs

4 teaspoons honey

2 x 125 g tubs low-fat vanilla yoghurt

Preheat grill to high. Cut each fig in half, place the figs on an ovenproof tray, cut side up and drizzle the honey over the figs.

Grill the figs for 2–3 minutes or until slightly caramelised. To serve, place three fig halves on four serving plates, top with a spoon of the yoghurt. Serve immediately.

TIP *These figs are also great with maple syrup instead of honey.*

425 kj
Fat 0.4 g
Saturated fat 0.1 g
Carbohydrates 17.0 g
Protein 6.0 g
Sugars 17.1 g
Fibre 1.0 g

PER SERVE

CARAMEL & BANANA TART

This mouth-watering dessert tart is surprisingly easy to prepare with a shortcut sponge base and a creamy caramel and banana topping.

SERVES 8 | PREPARATION 15 MINUTES | COOKING 30 MINUTES

melted butter, to grease

1 half of bought 17 cm unfilled sponge cake, halved horizontally

⅓ cup firmly packed dark brown sugar, plus 2 teaspoons extra

1 egg

3 eggwhites

310 ml (1¼ cups) reduced-fat milk

1 teaspoon vanilla essence

2 ripe bananas

¼ cup finely chopped pitted dried dates

80 ml (⅓ cup) reduced-fat thickened cream

Preheat oven to 180°C or 160°C fan-forced. Lightly brush an 18-cm pie plate with the melted butter.

Place the sponge half between two sheets of baking paper and roll with a rolling pin until flattened. Place the rolled sponge cake in the base of the prepared pie plate. Place the pie plate on a baking tray.

Whisk the brown sugar, egg and eggwhites together until combined. Gradually whisk in the milk and vanilla essence until well combined.

Cut the bananas on the diagonal into slices 3 mm thick. Arrange the slices, slightly overlapping, over the sponge base and sprinkle with the dates. Pour the egg mixture over the banana and dates.

Bake the tart for 20 minutes. Sprinkle with the extra brown sugar and bake for a further 10 minutes or until a round-bladed knife comes out clean when inserted in the centre of the tart.

Serve the tart warm or at room temperature. Cut into wedges and serve drizzled with the cream.

TIP *Use the remaining sponge half for another dessert, such as trifle.*

904 kj
Fat 6.6 g
Saturated fat 3.7 g
Carbohydrates 34.1 g
Protein 6.2 g
Sugars 28.7 g
Fibre 1.5 g

PER SERVE

BURNT HONEY, ORANGE & YOGHURT PANNA COTTA

Master the art of the delicate panna cotta and whip up heavenly, airy desserts like a pro.

SERVES 8 | PREPARATION 20 MINUTES + COOLING AND SETTING TIME | COOKING 10 MINUTES

vegetable oil, to grease

185 ml (¾ cup) honey

125 ml (½ cup) fresh orange juice

2 x 500 g cartons Greek-style yoghurt

1 tablespoon orange flower water (optional)

3 teaspoons powdered gelatine

2 x 250 g punnets strawberries, halved

1 tablespoon caster sugar

1 teaspoon freshly ground black pepper

Lightly grease eight 200-ml dariole moulds. Bring the honey to the boil in a saucepan over high heat. Cook for 3–4 minutes or until deep golden. Immediately remove from the heat and stir in the orange juice. Return to the heat and cook, stirring, for 1–2 minutes or until smooth. Set aside for 1 hour to cool.

1194 kj
Fat 9.2 g
Saturated fat 5.6 g
Carbohydrates 43.2 g
Protein 7.5 g
Sugars 43.2 g
Fibre 1.5 g

PER SERVE

Combine the yoghurt and orange flower water in a bowl. Add the cooled honey mixture and stir until well combined.

Put 60 ml (¼ cup) water in a small saucepan and sprinkle with the gelatine. Set aside for 5 minutes to soak. Place over low heat and cook, stirring, for 1–2 minutes or until the gelatine dissolves. Remove from the heat. Add 2–3 tablespoons of the yoghurt mixture and stir to combine. Add the gelatine mixture to the remaining yoghurt mixture and combine. Pour into the prepared moulds. Place on a tray and cover with plastic wrap. Place in the fridge for 6 hours or overnight to set.

Combine the strawberries, sugar and pepper in a bowl. Set aside for 15 minutes to develop the flavours.

Dip the moulds, one at a time, into hot water for 1–2 seconds, then turn out into serving bowls. Serve immediately with the black pepper strawberries.

RHUBARB & GINGER CRUMBLE

Did you know rhubarb is in fact a vegetable? Rhubarb is available all year round, but grows best in cooler months. Keep this recipe for a special occasion.

SERVES 4 | PREPARATION 10 MINUTES | COOKING 30–35 MINUTES

300 g (about 2) green apples, peeled, cored and cut into thin wedges
350 g rhubarb, trimmed, cut into 4 cm lengths
1 tablespoon caster sugar
½ teaspoon finely grated lemon zest

Crumble

¼ cup plain flour
2 tablespoons reduced-fat margarine
70 g rolled oats
1½ tablespoons brown sugar
½ teaspoon ground ginger

Preheat oven to 180°c or 160°c fan-forced. Lightly grease a 1-litre (4-cup) ovenproof dish.

Place the apples, rhubarb, 80 ml (⅓ cup) water, the sugar and lemon zest in a saucepan and simmer for 10–15 minutes, or until the apples and rhubarb are just tender.

Meanwhile, place the flour in a bowl. Using clean fingers, rub the margarine into the flour until well combined and large crumbs form. Mix in the oats, sugar and ginger.

Spoon the fruit into the dish, sprinkle the topping evenly over the fruit. Bake for 20 minutes or until golden and bubbling.

750 kj
Fat 6.0 g
Saturated fat 0.8 g
Carbohydrates 27.0 g
Protein 2.7 g
Sugars 18.9 g
Fibre 4.9 g

PER SERVE

CARROT & CINNAMON CAKE

Relax with a hot cup of tea and a generous slice of this low-fat carrot cake.

SERVES 8 | PREPARATION 15 MINUTES | COOKING 45 MINUTES

- melted butter, to grease
- 1 cup self-raising flour
- ½ cup wholemeal self-raising flour
- 2 teaspoons ground cinnamon, plus ¼ teaspoon extra
- ¾ cup firmly packed brown sugar
- 125 ml (½ cup) reduced-fat milk
- 60 ml (¼ cup) vegetable oil
- 2 eggs, lightly whisked
- 240 g (about 2 large) carrots, peeled and finely shredded
- 1 tablespoon icing sugar

1141 kj
Fat 8.9 g
Saturated fat 1.5 g
Carbohydrates 42.1 g
Protein 5.5 g
Sugars 22.7 g
Fibre 3.0 g

PER SERVE

Preheat oven to 180°C or 160°C fan-forced. Lightly brush a 20-cm round cake tin with the melted butter. Line the base with baking paper.

Sift the flours and cinnamon into a bowl and add the husks to the bowl. Stir in the sugar. Whisk the milk, oil and eggs together. Add to the flour mixture and use a wooden spoon to mix until well combined and smooth. Stir in the carrot until just combined.

Pour the mixture into the prepared tin and bake for 45 minutes or until a skewer inserted in the centre comes out clean. Set aside for 5 minutes and then turn onto a wire rack to cool.

Combine the icing sugar and extra cinnamon in a small bowl. Sift over the cooled cake before cutting into wedges to serve.

TIP *Keep this cake in an airtight container in the fridge for up to a day and serve at room temperature.*

AUTUMN FRUITS IN POMEGRANATE SYRUP

Enjoy the fruits of the season with this easy, low-fat dessert recipe.

SERVES 4 | PREPARATION 10 MINUTES | COOKING 10 MINUTES

2 starfruit, sliced

3 nashi pears, cored and cut into wedges

6 passionfruit, pulp removed

3 pomegranates, halved, juiced with citrus juicer

2 tablespoons caster sugar

Place the starfruit, pears and passionfruit pulp in a large bowl. Toss to combine.

Place the pomegranate juice and caster sugar in a small saucepan. Stir over medium heat for 3 minutes or until the sugar dissolves. Bring to the boil, then reduce the heat and simmer, uncovered, for 3 minutes. Remove from the heat and set aside for 5 minutes.

Pour the syrup over the fruit and toss gently to combine. Serve immediately.

TIP *You can heat the pomegranate juice in the microwave if you prefer. Place the pomegranate juice and caster sugar in a heat-resistant, microwave-safe jug or bowl. Cook, uncovered, stirring twice, for 4 minutes on medium–high/650 watts/70%.*

960 kj
Fat 0.6 g
Saturated fat 0.1 g
Carbohydrates 49.6 g
Protein 5.0 g
Sugars 48.8 g
Fibre 17.8 g

PER SERVE

FILO ROLLS WITH COTTAGE CHEESE & CHERRIES

Filo pastry has less than 1 g of fat per sheet compared to puff pastry, which contains more than 25 g of fat per sheet. Look after your family's heart health by using filo pastry in sweet and savoury recipes.

SERVES 4 | PREPARATION 10 MINUTES | COOKING 15–20 MINUTES

425 g tin pitted black cherries, drained
⅓ cup low-fat cottage cheese
1 tablespoon brown sugar
¼ teaspoon ground cinnamon
4 sheets filo pastry
olive oil spray
icing sugar, to dust

Preheat oven to 180°C or 160°C fan-forced. Place the cherries on a large plate lined with absorbent paper and set aside for 10 minutes to absorb any excess juice.

Place the cherries, cottage cheese, brown sugar and cinnamon in a mixing bowl and stir to combine. Working on a clean work surface, cut each sheet of filo in half to give eight pieces.

Take a piece of filo, spray lightly with olive oil and fold in half. Place one-eighth of the cherry filling at the short end closest to you, leaving a 2 cm border. Fold the filo over to enclose the filling, then tuck in the edges and continue to roll to form a cigar shape. Spray with a little more oil and place on a baking tray lined with baking paper. Repeat with the remaining filo and filling to make eight rolls.

Bake in the preheated oven for 15–20 minutes or until golden. Serve immediately, dusted with a little icing sugar.

TIP *Filo rolls will become soft on standing, so it's best to eat them immediately.*

630 kj
Fat 0.6 g
Saturated fat 0.2 g
Carbohydrates 30.0 g
Protein 5.6 g
Sugars 21 g
Fibre 2.1 g

PER SERVE

BABY BANANA CHEESECAKES

Treat yourself with these indulgent little banana cheesecakes, which are lower in fat and kilojoules compared to regular cheesecake.

SERVES 4 | PREPARATION 15 MINUTES | COOKING 30 MINUTES + COOLING TIME

canola oil spray
4 shredded wheatmeal biscuits
2 tablespoons hazelnut meal
30 g butter, melted
150 g fresh ricotta
40 g light cream cheese
2 tablespoons brown sugar
½ teaspoon vanilla essence
100 g ripe banana (about half a banana), peeled and mashed
1 egg
grated dark chocolate, to serve

Spray four holes of a 125-ml (½-cup) muffin tray with oil. Line each hole in a cross pattern with two 15 cm strips of baking paper.

Place the biscuits in a bowl and crush into fine crumbs. Stir in the hazelnut meal and melted butter. Divide the mixture among the muffin holes, and press it into the base of each. Refrigerate for 20 minutes.

Preheat oven to 180°C or 160°C fan-forced. Beat the ricotta, cream cheese, sugar and vanilla essence until smooth. Beat in the banana and egg. Pour the mixture over the biscuit bases. Bake for 30 minutes, then turn the oven off and leave the cheesecakes in the oven with the door ajar for 1 hour. Refrigerate for 30 minutes. Sprinkle with grated chocolate to serve.

1368 kj
Fat 22.4 g
Saturated fat 10.5 g
Carbohydrates 23.0 g
Protein 9.5 g
Sugars 17.2 g
Fibre 2.4 g

PER SERVE

BAKED APPLES

An apple a day is easy if you have them in this delicious baked apple dessert.

SERVES 4 | PREPARATION 15 MINUTES | COOKING 30 MINUTES

4 apples (such as Golden Delicious or Granny Smith)
1 tablespoon lemon juice
⅓ cup sultanas
2 teaspoons vanilla essence
2 tablespoons brown sugar
2 tablespoons slivered almonds, toasted
1 teaspoon mixed spice
low-fat custard, to serve

Preheat oven to 180°C or 160°C fan-forced. Using a small sharp knife, remove the cores from the apples, leaving the apples whole and the bases intact. (Alternatively, an apple corer makes this job a little easier.) Slice around the middle of each apple skin to prevent them bursting during cooking.

Drizzle the lemon juice into the apple cavities. Place the apples upright into a ceramic baking dish.

Combine the sultanas, vanilla essence, sugar, almonds and mixed spice. Spoon the sultana mixture into the centre of each apple. Cover with foil. Bake for 15 minutes, then remove the foil. Bake for a further 10–15 minutes or until the apples are tender. Serve warm with custard.

TIP *Keep a close eye on the apples, as cooking time will vary depending on the size of the apples.*

842 kj
Fat 3.6 g
Saturated fat 0.4 g
Carbohydrates 37.2 g
Protein 3.1 g
Sugars 35.1 g
Fibre 5.0 g

PER SERVE

CARAMELISED FRUIT KEBABS

Kids will love helping to prepare this tasty treat. Served warm, these kebabs are a great new way to enjoy the goodness of fruit.

SERVES 4 | PREPARATION 10 MINUTES | COOKING 5 MINUTES

1 tablespoon orange juice

1½ tablespoons brown sugar

250 g small strawberries, halved if large

½ small pineapple, peeled, cored and cut into 2 cm chunks

2 small or 1 large firm ripe banana, cut into 2 cm rounds

Place the orange juice and sugar in a large bowl and stir to combine. Add the strawberries, pineapple and banana and gently stir to coat in the sugar mixture.

Preheat grill on high. Thread the fruit alternately on eight small wooden skewers (soaked in cold water) or metal skewers. Place the fruit kebabs on a baking tray and grill for 3–4 minutes, turning occasionally, or until the fruit is golden, tender and slightly caramelised.

TIP *You are less likely to eat unhealthy snacks if you keep a piece of fruit handy. Pack an extra piece in your lunch box or work bag, leave an apple in your handbag, or an orange in your car to grab when hunger strikes.*

360 kj
Fat 0.1 g
Saturated fat 0.0 g
Carbohydrates 17.5 g
Protein 2.0 g
Sugars 16.6 g
Fibre 3.3 g

PER SERVE

BAKED BLUEBERRY & PEACH MERINGUES

These fruit desserts look impressive but they are very quick and easy to make.

SERVES 4 | PREPARATION 15 MINUTES | COOKING 10 MINUTES

2 eggwhites, at room temperature

½ cup caster sugar

250 g drained tinned peaches (in natural juice)

1 cup thawed frozen blueberries

2 tablespoons almond meal

Preheat oven to 220°C or 200°C fan-forced. Using an electric beater, whisk the eggwhites in a clean, dry bowl until firm peaks form. Add the sugar, 1 tablespoon at a time, beating well after each addition until the sugar dissolves and the mixture is thick and glossy.

Combine the peaches, blueberries and almond meal in a bowl. Spoon the fruit mixture among four 185-ml (¾-cup) ramekins and top with a dollop of meringue. Bake for 7–10 minutes or until the meringue is golden. Serve immediately.

719 kj
Fat 2.4 g
Saturated fat 0.2 g
Carbohydrates 34.4 g
Protein 3.3 g
Sugars 33.5 g
Fibre 1.8 g

PER SERVE

BUTTERMILK PUDDING WITH SPICED CHERRIES

Traditional buttermilk pudding is given a decadent boost with the addition of spiced cherries.

SERVES 4 | PREPARATION 15 MINUTES + SETTING TIME | COOKING 5 MINUTES

1 vanilla bean

500 ml (2 cups) buttermilk

½ cup caster sugar

1 tablespoon boiling water

2½ teaspoons gelatine powder

½ cup caster sugar, plus extra

2 cinnamon sticks

3 star anise (optional)

400 g cherries

Cut the vanilla bean in half lengthwise and scrape out the seeds. Put the seeds in a saucepan with the buttermilk and sugar. Warm over low heat to dissolve the sugar, but do not boil.

Put the boiling water in a small bowl, sprinkle over the gelatine and whisk to combine, then whisk quickly into the warm buttermilk. Let cool, whisking occasionally, then pour the buttermilk mixture into four 125-ml (½-cup) dariole moulds. Refrigerate overnight.

Put the extra sugar, 185 ml (¾ cup) water, cinnamon and star anise (if using) in a saucepan and bring to the boil, stirring occasionally, until the sugar dissolves. Remove the pan from the heat and add the cherries. Set aside to cool.

Turn the puddings out onto serving plates by placing the base in hot water for a few seconds. Serve with the spiced cherries.

1509 kj
Fat 2.8 g
Saturated fat 1.7 g
Carbohydrates 76.6 g
Protein 8.2 g
Sugars 75.0 g
Fibre 2.0 g

PER SERVE

BERRY MERINGUE NESTS

By simply replacing cream with low-fat yoghurt this recipe cuts out the saturated fat from a family favourite desert – the Pavlova!

SERVES 4 | PREPARATION 10 MINUTES | COOKING NIL

125 g fresh raspberries

125 g fresh blueberries

1 tablespoon Frangelico (optional)

4 meringue nests

⅔ cup low-fat vanilla yoghurt

Place the raspberries and blueberries in a bowl, add the Frangelico, stir to combine and set aside to macerate for 5 minutes.

Place the meringue nests on four small serving plates. Top each nest with 2 tablespoons of the vanilla yoghurt, then a spoonful of the berries.

Serve immediately.

TIP *You could substitute the Frangelico with orange juice.*

730 kj
Fat 1.4 g
Saturated fat 0.8 g
Carbohydrates 34.0 g
Protein 4.0 g
Sugars 33.7 g
Fibre 2.2 g

PER SERVE

POACHED PEACHES WITH CINNAMON & HONEY RICOTTA

When peaches aren't in season use canned peaches instead – choose the ones in fruit juice rather than syrup. You can also try this recipe with nectarines or apricots depending on what's in season.

SERVES 4 | PREPARATION 10 MINUTES | COOKING 20 MINUTES

- ⅓ cup caster sugar
- 2 cinnamon sticks
- 4 large firm ripe freestone peaches
- 125 g (½ cup) low-fat ricotta
- 2 teaspoons honey
- ¼ teaspoon ground cinnamon

Place 1 litre (4 cups) water, sugar and the cinnamon sticks in a saucepan and cook stirring over medium heat until the sugar dissolves. Simmer for 5 minutes.

Add the peaches and poach for a further 5 minutes. Remove the peaches with a slotted spoon and peel away the skins. Simmer the syrup until reduced to one-third and strain.

Meanwhile, combine the ricotta, honey and ground cinnamon, then set aside. Serve the peaches drizzled with a little of the syrup and a dollop of the cinnamon and honey ricotta.

800 kj
Fat 3.0 g
Saturated fat 1.8 g
Carbohydrates 25.0 g
Protein 5.0 g
Sugars 34.3 g
Fibre 2.6 g

PER SERVE

RHUBARB AND YOGHURT FOOL

Don't let the name 'fool' you – this dessert is delicious!

SERVES 4 | PREPARATION 10 MINUTES + CHILLING | COOKING 10 MINUTES

1 bunch rhubarb, leaves discarded

2 tablespoons caster sugar

1 teaspoon ground nutmeg

600 g low-fat French vanilla yoghurt

8 pieces almond bread, to serve

Trim the rhubarb, wash well and cut into 1-cm pieces. Put the rhubarb in a saucepan over medium heat. Drizzle with 1 tablespoon water and add the sugar. Cover and bring to the boil. Remove the lid and simmer, stirring occasionally, for 5 minutes or until the rhubarb is soft and pulpy.

Transfer the rhubarb to a bowl and stir in the nutmeg. Cover and refrigerate for 1 hour or until chilled.

Layer the yoghurt and rhubarb mixture in small serving bowls, then swirl together with a spoon. Serve with the almond bread.

1336 kj
Fat 7.4 g
Saturated fat 3.3 g
Carbohydrates 47.4 g
Protein 12.2 g
Sugars 36.6 g
Fibre 3.5 g

PER SERVE

BALSAMIC ROASTED STRAWBERRIES

Only four ingredients are needed to create this gourmet roasted strawberry dessert.

SERVES 4 | PREPARATION 10 MINUTES + MARINATING TIME | COOKING 10 MINUTES

2 x 250 g punnets strawberries, washed and hulled

2 tablespoons caster sugar

1 tablespoon balsamic vinegar

thick natural yoghurt, to serve

Preheat oven to 200°C or 180°C fan-forced. Place the strawberries, sugar and vinegar in a shallow ovenproof dish, large enough to hold the strawberries in a single layer. Stir well to combine. Set aside for 20 minutes.

Roast the strawberries for 10 minutes or until just tender. Set aside to cool. Serve the strawberries and juices with the yoghurt.

418 kj
Fat 0.8 g
Saturated fat 0.4 g
Carbohydrates 16.9 g
Protein 4.7 g
Sugars 16.9 g
Fibre 2.6 g

PER SERVE

BERRY & MINT SORBET

A light, fruity dessert that is perfect on hot summer days.

SERVES 4 | PREPARATION 10 MINUTES + FREEZING | COOKING 5 MINUTES

½ cup caster sugar

¾ cup mixed berries

½ cup roughly chopped mint leaves

extra mint leaves to garnish

Heat sugar and 1¾ cups water in a saucepan, stirring occasionally until sugar dissolves. Bring to the boil over medium heat, add berries and cook for a couple of minutes until soft. Remove from the heat, add the mint leaves and allow to cool completely.

Strain the mixture through a sieve to remove all the berry seeds and pour into a plastic container. Freeze overnight.

534 kj
Fat 0.0 g
Saturated fat 0.0 g
Carbohydrates 32.0 g
Protein 0.6 g
Sugars 26.8 g
Fibre 1 g

PER SERVE

BANANA BREAD & BUTTER PUDDING

Would you like a few good reasons to try this new twist on an old favourite? It's low fat and really easy to make!

SERVES 4 | PREPARATION 20 MINUTES | COOKING 50 MINUTES

40 g reduced-fat dairy spread
9 slices oat bran and honey bread
500 ml (2 cups) skim milk
3 eggs
2 tablespoons yellow box honey (see Tip)
1 teaspoon ground cinnamon
2 small bananas, thinly sliced
low-fat ice cream or custard, to serve

Preheat oven to 170°C or 150°C fan-forced. Spread the reduced-fat spread over both sides of the slices of bread. Cut off the crusts and then cut each slice of bread in half.

Whisk the milk, eggs, honey and cinnamon together in a jug.

Layer the bread in a greased 1.25-litre (5-cup) ovenproof dish. Top with the banana slices. Pour over the milk mixture, then set aside for 10 minutes. Bake for 45–50 minutes or until puffed and golden. Serve with ice cream or custard.

TIP *Capilano makes a yellow box honey that is readily available from supermarkets. It has a smooth flavour and is well suited to Chinese cooking and as a baste for lamb and poultry.*

1855 kj
Fat 15.4 g
Saturated fat 6.3 g
Carbohydrates 57.1 g
Protein 20.3 g
Sugars 32.6 g
Fibre 6.3 g

PER SERVE

CARAMELISED RICOTTA & BLUEBERRY POTS

These little pots of perfection combine creamy ricotta with sweet blueberries.

SERVES 4 | PREPARATION 10 MINUTES | COOKING 10 MINUTES

200 g frozen blueberries

300 g fresh ricotta

2 tablespoons caster sugar

½ teaspoon vanilla essence

¼ cup raw (demerara) sugar

Place the frozen blueberries and 1 tablespoon water in a saucepan over medium heat. Cook, covered, for 3–4 minutes or until the blueberries have thawed completely and are heated through. Drain the liquid. Divide the blueberries among four 185-ml (¾-cup) heat-resistant dishes.

Preheat grill to high. Using electric beaters, beat the ricotta, caster sugar and vanilla in a bowl until smooth. Spoon the ricotta mixture evenly over the blueberries and use the back of the spoon to smooth the surface. Place the dishes on a large baking tray.

Sprinkle the raw sugar evenly over the top of the ricotta mixture. Place under the hot grill and cook for 3–5 minutes or until the sugar dissolves and becomes golden brown. Remove from the grill and stand for 5 minutes before serving.

919 kj
Fat 8.5 g
Saturated fat 5.4 g
Carbohydrates 28.7 g
Protein 8.2 g
Sugars 28.4 g
Fibre 0.9 g

PER SERVE

BLOOD ORANGE JELLY

Blood oranges are in season from July to early September. At other times of the year use the juice from navel or Valencia oranges.

SERVES 4 | PREPARATION 10 MINUTES + SETTING TIME | COOKING 5 MINUTES

2 cups freshly squeezed blood orange juice

¼ cup caster sugar

1 tablespoon gelatine powder

¼ cup hot water

2 oranges, segmented, to serve

Place the blood orange juice and sugar in a saucepan over medium heat. Stir until the sugar has dissolved, then simmer for 3 minutes.

Whisk together the gelatine and hot water until the gelatine has dissolved. Pour into the hot juice and stir to combine. Pour into four ½-cup or two 1-cup jelly moulds and refrigerate overnight to set.

To serve, dip each mould into warm water for 20 seconds to loosen the jellies and invert onto serving plates. Serve with orange segments.

550 kj
Fat 0.0 g
Saturated fat 0.0 g
Carbohydrates 28.0 g
Protein 4.1 g
Sugars 27.9 g
Fibre 1.6 g

PER SERVE

CASHEW CRUMBLE PEARS

Beurre bosc pears are the best choice to use in this recipe and are usually available between March and November each year.

SERVES 4 | PREPARATION 10 MINUTES | COOKING 20 MINUTES

¼ cup cashew nuts
30 g chilled unsalted butter, cubed
¼ cup self-raising flour
2 tablespoons brown sugar
4 ripe beurre bosc pears, halved and cored
¼ cup maple syrup
vanilla ice cream, to serve

Preheat oven to 180°C or 160°C fan-forced. Place the cashews on a baking tray and roast for 5 minutes or until golden. Chop, then set aside.

Use your fingertips to rub the butter into the flour. Stir in the sugar.

Brush the pears with the maple syrup. Place a frying pan over medium heat and cook the pears, in batches, for 1–2 minutes or until lightly golden. Transfer to a baking dish, cut side up.

Top the pears with the crumble mixture and scatter over the cashews. Bake for 10 minutes or until the crumble is golden. Serve with any remaining maple syrup and ice cream.

1388 kj
Fat 11.6 g
Saturated fat 5.3 g
Carbohydrates 55.3 g
Protein 4.0 g
Sugars 40.6 g
Fibre 4.2 g

PER SERVE

CARDAMOM ORANGES

This quick and easy orange dessert is the perfect low-kilojoule after-dinner dessert.

SERVES 4 | PREPARATION 5 MINUTES | COOKING 5 MINUTES

⅓ cup flaked almonds

5 oranges

2 tablespoons caster sugar

½ teaspoon ground cardamom

150 g carton reduced-fat natural yoghurt

Toast the almonds in a large non-stick frying pan over medium heat, stirring often, for 1–2 minutes or until light golden. Transfer to a plate.

Juice 1 of the oranges and reserve 60 ml (¼ cup) of the juice. Use a small sharp knife to remove the rind and white pith from the remaining oranges. Cut the oranges into slices 1 cm thick.

Combine the reserved orange juice, sugar and cardamom in the frying pan. Stir over low heat until the sugar dissolves, then increase the heat to high and bring to the boil. Boil, uncovered, for 30–60 seconds or until the liquid reduces and thickens slightly. Remove the pan from the heat. Add the orange slices and turn to coat in the syrup.

Place the orange slices on serving plates and drizzle with the syrup. Scatter the toasted almonds over the top and serve with yoghurt.

815 kj
Fat 4.6 g
Saturated fat 0.4 g
Carbohydrates 26.9 g
Protein 8.9 g
Sugars 26.8 g
Fibre 3.9 g

PER SERVE

INDIVIDUAL RASPBERRY TRIFLES

We used low-fat lemon biscuits for this recipe, but there are plenty of other varieties available at your supermarket.

SERVES 4 | PREPARATION 15 MINUTES | COOKING NIL

300 g low-fat vanilla yoghurt
½ cup low-fat pouring custard
4 low-fat lemon biscuits
4 meringue nests
250 g raspberries

Place the yoghurt and custard in a bowl and mix until smooth. Roughly chop the biscuits and meringues together.

Sprinkle a little of the combined biscuit and meringue mixture over the base of 4 serving glasses. Top with some raspberries and a dollop of the yoghurt mixture. Repeat the layers once more, finishing with raspberries. Refrigerate for 10 minutes before serving.

916 kj
Fat 4.0 g
Saturated fat 2.0 g
Carbohydrates 35.0 g
Protein 7.4 g
Sugars 44.6 g
Fibre 3.6 g

PER SERVE

HONEY-BAKED PEARS WITH RICOTTA

Easy and tasty, these delicious treats are the perfect indulgence.

SERVES 4 | PREPARATION 15 MINUTES | COOKING 25 MINUTES

- 4 firm, ripe pears, halved, leaving stems intact
- 200 g low-fat fresh ricotta
- 2 tablespoons honey
- 8 amaretti biscuits, roughly crushed

Preheat oven to 180°C or 160°C fan-forced. Line a baking tray with non-stick baking paper.

Use a teaspoon to scoop out the seeds and centre core of each pear half to make a round hollow. Place the pear halves on the lined tray. Spoon the ricotta into the hollows in the pear halves. Drizzle with honey and sprinkle with biscuit.

Bake for 25 minutes or until the pears are tender and the biscuit is golden brown. Divide the pear halves among serving plates. Drizzle with the remaining honey in the dish to serve.

1328 kj
Fat 9.4 g
Saturated fat 4.6 g
Carbohydrates 50.0 g
Protein 8.3 g
Sugars 35.8 g
Fibre 3.5 g

PER SERVE

CHARGRILLED MANGO WITH LIME & MINT SUGAR

Finish off your barbecue dinner with these luscious mangoes served with ice cream.

SERVES 4 | PREPARATION 5 MINUTES | COOKING 5 MINUTES

2 tablespoons sugar

finely grated zest of 1 lime

¼ cup mint leaves

2 mangoes

4 scoops low-fat ice cream, to serve

Put the sugar, lime zest and mint in the small bowl of a food processor and process until well combined.

Preheat a barbecue plate on medium–high. Using a sharp knife, cut 2 cheeks from each mango, cutting as close to the stone as possible. Line the barbecue plate with baking paper. Place the mango cheeks, flesh side down, on the baking paper and cook for 4–5 minutes or until golden.

Score 3 vertical lines and 3 horizontal lines into each mango cheek (don't cut all the way through). Turn the mango skin inside out. Place a mango cheek on each serving plate, sprinkle with the lime and mint sugar, and serve with ice cream.

TIP *Alternatively, the mango cheeks can be cooked in a frying pan. Use the baking paper in the same way as for the barbecuing method.*

530 kj
Fat 1.1 g
Saturated fat 0.5 g
Carbohydrates 26.6 g
Protein 2.3 g
Sugars 25.9 g
Fibre 1.9 g

PER SERVE

CHOCOLATE & BEETROOT CAKE WITH CARDAMOM FROSTING

Beetroot will deepen the colour of the chocolate cake as well as adding to the flavour.

SERVES 4 | PREPARATION 15 MINUTES | COOKING 1 HOUR

melted butter, to grease
200 g (about 2) trimmed beetroot bulbs
¼ cup cocoa powder
60 ml (¼ cup) hot water
1 cup firmly packed brown sugar
2 eggs, lightly whisked
125 ml (½ cup) reduced-fat milk
60 ml (¼ cup) vegetable oil
1 teaspoon vanilla essence
1½ cups self-raising flour, sifted

Cardamom frosting
1 cup pure icing sugar, sifted
pinch of ground cardamom
4½ teaspoons reduced-fat milk

1277 kj
Fat 8.3 g
Saturated fat 2.0 g
Carbohydrates 53.4 g
Protein 5.1 g
Sugars 36.8 g
Fibre 1.7 g
PER SERVE

Preheat oven to 180°C or 160°C fan-forced. Grease and line a 7-cm deep, 11 cm x 21 cm loaf tin with baking paper.

Peel the beetroot, then use a grater to finely shred them. Set aside.

Put the cocoa and hot water in a large bowl and stir until smooth. Add the sugar and eggs, and use a wooden spoon to beat until smooth. Stir in the beetroot.

Combine the milk, oil and vanilla in a jug. Use a spoon to fold half the flour and then half the milk mixture into the beetroot mixture until just combined. Repeat with the remaining mixtures.

Pour the cake mixture into the prepared tin. Bake for 55–60 minutes or until a skewer inserted into the centre of the cake comes out clean. Set aside for 5 minutes and then turn out onto a wire rack to cool.

To make the cardamom frosting, use a wooden spoon to mix the icing sugar, cardamom and milk in a small bowl until smooth. Spread over the top of the cooled cake and set aside for 15 minutes to set.

FAIRY CUPCAKES

These are best eaten on the day they are made.

MAKES 12 | PREPARATION 15 MINUTES | COOKING 15 MINUTES

2 eggs

2 tablespoons caster sugar

½ cup self-raising flour, sifted

½ teaspoon baking powder

2 tablespoons extra-light spreadable cream cheese

2 tablespoons low-fat custard

½ teaspoon caster sugar

½ teaspoon vanilla essence

¼ teaspoon cinnamon

icing sugar, for dusting

Preheat the oven to 180°C. Line a 12-hole patty tin with paper cases.

Using an electric mixer, beat the eggs and sugar until pale and creamy. Fold in the flour and baking powder until just combined. Spoon into the paper cases, until two-thirds full. Bake for 12–15 minutes, or until the cakes spring back when lightly pressed. Cool the cupcakes on a wire rack.

Mix together the cream cheese, custard, sugar, vanilla and cinnamon until smooth. Cut a disc from the top of each cupcake and fill with the cream cheese mixture. Replace the top and repeat with the remaining cakes. Dust with icing sugar before serving.

TIP *The nutritional information is per cupcake.*

227 kj
Fat 1.5 g
Saturated fat 0.7 g
Carbohydrates 8.0 g
Protein 2.0 g
Sugars 2.4 g
Fibre 0.2 g

PER CUPCAKE

BARBECUED CINNAMON PEACHES

These sweet grilled peaches are a quick and easy dessert after the summer barbecue.

SERVES 4 | PREPARATION 10 MINUTES | COOKING 5 MINUTES

2 tablespoons brown sugar
½ teaspoon ground cinnamon
8 peaches, halved, stones removed
olive oil, to grease
lemon sorbet, to serve

Combine the sugar and cinnamon in a small bowl. Place the peach halves, cut side up, onto a plate. Sprinkle with the sugar mixture and set aside for 5 minutes.

Preheat a chargrill or barbecue grill on medium–high. Lightly grease the grill with oil, then cook the peaches, cut side down, for 5 minutes, or until charred. Serve immediately with sorbet.

681 kj
Fat 0.3 g
Saturated fat 0.0 g
Carbohydrates 34.9 g
Protein 2.6 g
Sugars 34.3 g
Fibre 3.6 g

PER SERVE

FRUIT JELLIES

These jellies are made with apple juice, or you could try an adult version using sparkling wine instead.

SERVES 6 | PREPARATION 5 MINUTES + COOLING AND SETTING TIME | COOKING 5 MINUTES

625 ml (2½ cups) clear apple juice

1½ tablespoons powdered gelatine

2 kiwifruit, peeled and diced

250 g punnet strawberries, hulled and sliced

Put 185 ml (¾ cup) water, the apple juice and gelatine into a small saucepan over medium heat. Cook, stirring, for 5 minutes or until the liquid just comes to the boil. Transfer to a bowl, then set aside to cool for 30 minutes. Cover and refrigerate for 45 minutes or until the jelly just starts to set.

Combine the kiwifruit and strawberries. Spoon the fruit into six 125-ml (½-cup) glasses. Top with the jelly, then cover and refrigerate for a further 4 hours or until completely set.

TIP *These jellies are best made 6–8 hours before serving. If left for more than 24 hours, the kiwifruit will begin to soften the enzymes in the jelly.*

331 kj
Fat 0.1 g
Saturated fat 0.0 g
Carbohydrates 14.7 g
Protein 3.8 g
Sugars 14.7 g
Fibre 1.8 g

PER SERVE

APPLE & RHUBARB CRUMBLE

This oaty crumble is perfect on a cold winter's night.

SERVES 4 | PREPARATION 10 MINUTES | COOKING 20 MINUTES

4 cups stewed apple and rhubarb

3 tablespoons butter

½ cup rolled oats

¼ cup shredded coconut

2 tablespoons almond meal

¼ teaspoon cinnamon

Preheat oven to 180°C.

Divide the stewed apple and rhubarb evenly between 4 individual (1-cup capacity) ramekins.

Place the butter and half the oats in a food processor and process until the mixture is the consistency of breadcrumbs. Tip into a mixing bowl and add the rest of the oats, coconut, almond meal and cinnamon.

Spoon the crumble mix over the fruit and bake for 15–20 minutes until crisp and golden.

Remove from the oven and let stand for 5 minutes before serving. Delicious served with low-fat natural yoghurt.

1101 kj
Fat 19.4 g
Saturated fat 11.6 g
Carbohydrates 11.3 g
Protein 5.4 g
Sugars 23.4 g
Fibre 8.1 g

PER SERVE

FRESH FRUIT WITH STRAWBERRY SAUCE

The strawberry and balsamic vinegar sauce adds a delightful zing to this classic fruit salad.

SERVES 4 | PREPARATION 10 MINUTES | COOKING NIL

2 bananas, peeled and sliced

½ small rockmelon, peeled and sliced

2 slices fresh pineapple, peeled, each cut into 8 wedges

2 oranges, peeled and segmented

Strawberry sauce

250 g punnet ripe strawberries, hulled

¼ cup low-joule berry jam

2 teaspoons balsamic vinegar

To make the strawberry sauce, place the strawberries, jam and balsamic vinegar in a food processor or blender and process until smooth and well combined.

Arrange the banana, rockmelon, pineapple and orange segments in serving bowls or on a platter. Serve with the strawberry sauce spooned over.

611 kj
Fat 0.4 g
Saturated fat 0.0 g
Carbohydrates 32.4 g
Protein 3.4 g
Sugars 30.8 g
Fibre 6.1 g

PER SERVE

GINGER-INFUSED CITRUS FRUIT SALAD

Enjoy this citrus salad in winter, when citrus fruits are at their best.

SERVES 4 | PREPARATION 10 MINUTES | COOKING NIL

- 3 mandarins
- 2 ruby grapefruit
- 2 oranges
- 2 tangelos
- 2 tablespoons caster sugar
- 1 teaspoon finely grated ginger

Peel and segment the mandarins, removing as much pith as possible. Using a sharp knife, peel the grapefruit, oranges and tangelos, and remove the pith. Segment the fruit between the membranes over a bowl, reserving the juice. Place the fruit segments in a bowl.

Sprinkle the fruit with the sugar and ginger. Gently toss to combine, then cover and refrigerate until chilled. Spoon into glasses and serve.

TIP *Ruby grapefruit is also known as pink grapefruit; it has a pink-red blush on its orange skin.*

553 kj
Fat 0.5 g
Saturated fat 0.0 g
Carbohydrates 27.8 g
Protein 2.9 g
Sugars 27.7 g
Fibre 5.8 g

PER SERVE

APRICOT, GINGER & HONEY COOKIES

The kick of ginger makes these cookies extra special.

MAKES 18 COOKIES (3 PER SERVE) | PREPARATION 10 MINUTES | COOKING 20 MINUTES

1 cup plain flour
1 cup rolled oats
½ teaspoon baking powder
2 tablespoons brown sugar
100 g butter
¼ cup honey
rind of 1 orange, finely grated
1 egg
½ teaspoon vanilla essence
¼ cup finely diced dried apricots
2 tablespoons finely diced crystallised ginger

Preheat oven to 175°C.

Mix together the flour, oats, baking powder and sugar. In a small saucepan gently melt the butter and honey. Remove from heat and add the orange rind, egg and vanilla essence. Pour over the oat mixture and combine, adding the apricots and ginger.

Spoon onto a lined baking tray, leaving room between each. Press to flatten into 5 cm rounds, and bake in the oven for 20 minutes until golden brown.

1494 kj
Fat 17.0 g
Saturated fat 9.6 g
Carbohydrates 44.0 g
Protein 6.0 g
Sugars 17.0 g
Fibre 4.1 g

PER SERVE

CHOCOLATE FUDGE CAKE WITH TOFU

Using tofu in place of additional chocolate gives this cake a deliciously fudgy texture.

SERVES 8 | PREPARATION 20 MINUTES | COOKING 45 MINUTES

vegetable oil spray
200 g silken firm tofu, drained
½ cup caster sugar
2 egg yolks
2 teaspoons vanilla essence
80 g dark chocolate (70% cocoa), melted
⅓ cup plain flour, sifted
1 tablespoon self-raising flour, sifted
4 eggwhites
low-fat vanilla yoghurt, to serve
raspberries, to serve (optional)
cocoa powder, to dust

759 kj
Fat 5.0 g
Saturated fat 2.3 g
Carbohydrates 30.0 g
Protein 6.5 g
Sugars 20.9 g
Fibre 1.2 g

PER SERVE

Preheat oven to 160°C or 140°C fan-forced. Spray a round 20-cm cake tin with vegetable oil. Line the base and side with non-stick baking paper.

Process the tofu, sugar, egg yolks and vanilla in a food processor until smooth. Add the chocolate and process until smooth. Transfer to a bowl and fold in the combined flours.

Beat the egg-whites with an electric beater in a clean, dry bowl until soft peaks form. Fold one-third of the egg-white into the chocolate mixture with a large metal spoon until just combined. Repeat, in two more batches, with the remaining eggwhite. Spoon the cake mixture into the prepared tin and smooth the surface. Bake for 40–45 minutes or until a skewer inserted into the centre of the cake comes out clean. Set aside in the tin to cool.

Cut the cake into slices. Top with yoghurt and raspberries and dust with cocoa powder.

GUILT-FREE VANILLA ICE CREAM

Real vanilla is the secret to this delicious ice cream.

SERVES 6 | PREPARATION 15 MINUTES + COOLING AND FREEZING TIME | COOKING 5 MINUTES

2 teaspoons powdered gelatine

375 ml light evaporated milk

1 vanilla bean, split

80 ml (⅓ cup) light thickened cream

Sprinkle the gelatine over 60 ml (¼ cup) cold water in a small heatproof jug. Place the jug in a small saucepan of simmering water and whisk with a fork until the gelatine dissolves. Set aside for 2 minutes to cool slightly.

Combine the evaporated milk and vanilla bean in a saucepan and bring to the boil over medium heat. Remove from the heat and stir in the gelatine mixture. Set aside for 15 minutes to cool.

Use an electric beater to whisk the cream in a small bowl until frothy.

Remove the vanilla bean from the milk mixture using kitchen tongs. Use a sharp knife to scrape seeds from vanilla bean into the milk mixture, then discard the bean. Use an electric beater to whisk the milk mixture in a large bowl until frothy. Gradually pour in the cream and whisk until combined.

Pour the mixture into a 2-litre (8-cup) shallow metal container. Cover with foil and place in the freezer for 3 hours or until just set.

Roughly break up the ice cream with a large metal spoon and transfer to a bowl. Beat with an electric beater until smooth and doubled in size, then quickly return to the container. Cover with foil and freeze for another 4 hours or until firm. Scoop into serving glasses or small bowls to serve.

334 kj
Fat 2.7 g
Saturated fat 1.8 g
Carbohydrates 7.7 g
Protein 6.5 g
Sugars 7.7 g
Fibre 0.0 g

PER SERVE

CARROT, SULTANA & WALNUT MUFFINS

Low in fat but high in flavour, these muffins make a great morning or afternoon snack.

MAKES 10 MUFFINS | PREPARATION 5 MINUTES | COOKING 20 MINUTES

1 cup wholemeal self-raising flour
¾ cup self-raising flour
⅓ cup brown sugar
1½ teaspoons ground cinnamon
¾ cup orange juice
2 tablespoons light sour cream
1 egg
½ cup finely grated carrot
⅓ cup sultanas
2 tablespoons chopped walnuts

Preheat oven to 180°C.

Mix both types of flour, sugar and cinnamon in a large bowl. In a separate bowl combine orange juice, sour cream and egg.

Fold the mixture into the flour, add carrot, sultanas and walnuts and stir until well combined. Spoon into a greased muffin tin and bake for 20 minutes until golden and firm to the touch.

805 kj
Fat 3.3 g
Saturated fat 0.9 g
Carbohydrates 33.2 g
Protein 5.4 g
Sugars 4.7 g
Fibre 3.8 g

PER MUFFIN

RED FRUIT SALAD WITH MINT SYRUP

Enjoy this refreshing dessert that doesn't take forever to prepare and goes down a treat with guests.

SERVES 4 | PREPARATION 10 MINUTES | COOKING 15 MINUTES

⅓ cup caster sugar
10 large mint leaves
250 g strawberries, halved
125 g raspberries
400 g watermelon, cut into 2.5 cm cubes

Put the sugar and 125 ml (½ cup) warm water in a small saucepan over low heat. Cook, stirring, for 3 minutes or until the sugar has dissolved. Add 8 mint leaves and increase the heat to medium. Simmer, without stirring, for 8 minutes or until the mixture thickens. Discard the mint leaves. Set the syrup aside to cool.

Finely shred the remaining mint leaves. Put the strawberries, raspberries and watermelon in a large bowl and toss to combine. Divide the fruit among four bowls and drizzle with the mint syrup. Sprinkle with the shredded mint to serve.

TIP *You could use pitted cherries instead of the raspberries.*

512 kj
Fat 0.4 g
Saturated fat 0.0 g
Carbohydrates 26.4 g
Protein 1.8 g
Sugars 26.2 g
Fibre 3.8 g
PER SERVE

HONEY & CINNAMON PEARS

Enjoy beurre bosc pears to the fullest with this tasty dessert.

SERVES 4 | PREPARATION 15 MINUTES | COOKING 35 MINUTES

1 sheet filo pastry
olive oil spray
3 large (800 g) beurre bosc pears, unpeeled, quartered, core removed
juice of 2 oranges
2 tablespoons honey
¼ teaspoon ground cinnamon, plus ¼ extra

Preheat oven to 180°C or 160°C fan-forced. Line 2 baking trays with baking paper.

Cut the filo pastry in half to form 2 sheets. Spray 1 sheet with oil, then top with the remaining sheet and spray with oil. Cut the pastry into 8 triangles. Place them in a single layer on the prepared trays. Bake for 5 minutes or until golden, swapping the trays over in the oven after 3 minutes. Remove from the oven and set aside. Increase the oven to 220°C or 200°C fan-forced.

Meanwhile, place the pears in a shallow baking dish. Combine 80 ml (⅓ cup) orange juice, the honey and ¼ teaspoon cinnamon in a microwave-safe jug. Microwave, uncovered, on high (100%) for 1 minute or until the honey melts. Pour the honey mixture over the pears.

Bake the pears, turning once, for 25 minutes or until the liquid starts to thicken and becomes slightly syrupy, and the pears are tender but holding their shape. Divide the pears among serving plates and drizzle with the honey mixture. Top with the pastry triangles and sprinkle with the remaining cinnamon.

809 kj
Fat 0.1 g
Saturated fat 0.0 g
Carbohydrates 45.5 g
Protein 1.2 g
Sugars 35.8 g
Fibre 5.5 g

PER SERVE

TIP *Beurre bosc is a readily available pear, with a cinnamon-brown skin and long, tapering neck. Its firm, juicy flesh makes it ideal for roasting, grilling and poaching.*

LEMON & HONEY BAKED RICOTTA

Fresh peaches are the icing on this delicious dessert that's so good you won't have to worry about what to do with any leftovers. It's the ideal sweet treat to pack for a picnic.

SERVES 6 | PREPARATION 15 MINUTES + COOLING TIME | COOKING 40 MINUTES

olive oil spray
500 g fresh ricotta
1 cup Greek-style yoghurt
1 tablespoon finely grated lemon zest
60 ml (¼ cup) lemon juice
½ cup honey
3 eggs, lightly whisked
½ teaspoon ground cinnamon
fresh peaches, to serve

Preheat oven to 180°C or 160°C fan-forced. Spray a 9 cm x 23 cm loaf tin with oil to lightly grease.

Use an electric beater to beat together the ricotta, yoghurt, lemon zest, lemon juice, honey, egg and cinnamon in a large bowl until smooth. Pour the ricotta mixture into the prepared tin. Bake for 35–40 minutes or until firm. Set aside for 30 minutes to cool.

Cut the peaches in half. Remove the stones and cut into wedges. Serve the ricotta in slices topped with some peaches.

1405 kj
Fat 16.0 g
Saturated fat 9.1 g
Carbohydrates 34.8 g
Protein 14.7 g
Sugars 34.6 g
Fibre 1.3 g

PER SERVE

APRICOT UPSIDE-DOWN CAKE

Upside-down cakes are known for their moist texture, and this one certainly confirms that.

SERVES 16 | PREPARATION 10 MINUTES | COOKING 40 MINUTES

vegetable or canola oil spray

2 tablespoons low-kilojoule apricot jam

1 x 410 g can unsweetened apricot halves, drained

2 eggs

½ cup caster sugar

¾ cup Light & Creamy Evaporated Milk

1 teaspoon vanilla essence

1½ cups self-raising flour, sifted

icing sugar, for dusting

Preheat the oven to 180°C. Spray a 18 x 26 cm baking tray with oil and line the base with baking paper.

Heat the jam in the microwave for 20 seconds on high and mix until smooth. Spread over the base of the prepared pan and top with the apricot halves.

Using an electric mixer, beat the eggs and sugar until pale and creamy. Add the evaporated milk and vanilla and beat well. Fold in the flour and mix gently to combine. Pour into the prepared baking tray, being careful not to disturb the apricots. Bake for 35 minutes, or until cooked when tested with a skewer.

Cool in the pan for 5 minutes before turning onto a serving plate. Dust with icing sugar before serving.

458 kj
Fat 1.0 g
Saturated fat 0.4 g
Carbohydrates 21.0 g
Protein 3.7 g
Sugars 11.9 g
Fibre 1 g

PER SERVE

LIME DELICIOUS

This is a surprising twist to the classic lemon delicious!

SERVES 4 | PREPARATION 10 MINUTES | COOKING 30 MINUTES

reduced-fat dairy spread, melted, to grease

2 eggs, separated

⅓ cup caster sugar

2 teaspoons finely grated lime zest

60 ml (¼ cup) lime juice

1 tablespoon reduced-fat dairy spread, extra, melted

250 ml (1 cup) light soy milk or rice milk

½ cup self-raising flour, sifted

2 eggwhites

Preheat oven to 180°C or 160°C fan-forced. Brush four shallow 250-ml (1-cup) ovenproof dishes with melted dairy spread to lightly grease. Place on a baking tray.

Whisk the egg yolks, sugar, lime zest, lime juice and extra melted dairy spread together in a bowl. Stir in the soy or rice milk and flour.

Use an electric beater to whisk the 4 eggwhites in a clean, dry bowl until soft peaks form. Use a metal spoon to fold the eggwhite into the lime mixture until just combined. Pour the mixture into the prepared dishes. Bake for 15 minutes or until set and lightly browned on top (the desserts will remain saucy underneath). Serve immediately.

1043 kj
Fat 7.7 g
Saturated fat 2.6 g
Carbohydrates 37.8 g
Protein 7.5 g
Sugars 21.2 g
Fibre 1.0 g

PER SERVE

LIME MERINGUE TARTS

Perfect for an after-dinner dessert, these lime meringue tarts taste as good as they look. And best of all, they are lower in fat, too.

SERVES 6 | PREPARATION 20 MINUTES + COOLING TIME | COOKING 25 MINUTES

4 sheets filo pastry

10 g light pro-activ spread (Flora brand), melted, plus 30 g extra

½ cup cornflour

1 cup caster sugar, plus ½ cup extra

80 ml (⅓ cup) lime juice

1 teaspoon finely grated lime zest

1 egg yolk

2–3 drops green liquid food colouring

3 eggwhites

Preheat oven to 180°C. Lay the filo pastry on a clean work surface, and cover the pastry with a dry tea towel, then a damp tea towel. Brush 1 sheet of filo with a little melted spread. Top with another sheet and continue layering with the remaining filo and spread. Cut the filo stack into 6 equal portions.

1317 kj
Fat 4.3 g
Saturated fat 0.9 g
Carbohydrates 67.6 g
Protein 3.2 g
Sugars 52.9 g
Fibre 0.3 g

PER SERVE

Line six round 8-cm fluted tart tins, with removable bases, with a portion of pastry and trim any excess. Place on a baking tray and bake for 10 minutes or until golden. Remove from the oven and set aside for 15 minutes to cool.

Meanwhile, combine the cornflour and sugar in a saucepan. Gradually stir in 310 ml (1¼ cups) cold water and the lime juice until smooth. Cook over medium heat, stirring with a wooden spoon, for 10 minutes or until the mixture boils and thickens. Remove from the heat. Stir in the lime zest, egg yolk, extra spread and food colouring. Cover with plastic wrap and set aside for 30 minutes. Spoon the lime mixture into the pastry and smooth the surface.

Whisk the eggwhites in a clean, dry bowl until soft peaks form. Gradually add the extra sugar and whisk until thick and glossy. Spoon the meringue on top of the tarts. Create small peaks on the meringue using the back of the spoon. Bake until the meringue is slightly crisp. Remove from the tart tins and serve immediately.

CHOCOLATE MOUSSE

When beating eggwhites it is important to use a clean, dry bowl, as any moisture will prevent them from forming soft peaks.

SERVES 4 | PREPARATION 10 MINUTES + COOLING | COOKING NIL

2 eggwhites
80 g dark chocolate, melted and cooled
400 g low-fat vanilla yoghurt

Using an electric mixer, beat the eggwhites until soft peaks form. Gradually add the chocolate, beating constantly until smooth and well combined. Fold in the yoghurt.

Spoon into small serving bowls and refrigerate overnight to set.

785 kj
Fat 6.3 g
Saturated fat 5.6 g
Carbohydrates 23.6 g
Protein 8.4 g
Sugars 23.8 g
Fibre 0.9 g

PER SERVE

LOW-FAT BAKED CUSTARD

Delight your guests with these baked custards, served in individual ramekins!

SERVES 4 | PREPARATION 10 MINUTES | COOKING 1 HOUR 5 MINUTES

2 eggs

1 eggwhite

1 teaspoon vanilla extract

¼ cup caster sugar

500 ml (2 cups) skim milk

¼ teaspoon ground nutmeg

565 kj
Fat 2.7 g
Saturated fat 0.9 g
Carbohydrates 19.6 g
Protein 8.8 g
Sugars 19.6 g
Fibre 0.0 g

PER SERVE

Preheat oven to 160°C or 140°C fan-forced. Using a balloon whisk, whisk the eggs, eggwhite, vanilla and sugar in a bowl until well combined but not frothy.

Heat the milk in a saucepan over low heat for 3–4 minutes or until hot (do not boil). Pour the milk in a thin, steady stream over the egg mixture, whisking constantly until well combined. Strain the custard through a fine sieve (this is to prevent strands of egg forming in the custard).

Pour the strained custard into four 185-ml (¾-cup) ramekins. Place the ramekins in a baking dish. Sprinkle nutmeg over the top of the custards. Pour enough boiling water into the baking dish so it comes halfway up the sides of the ramekins (this is known as a water bath). Bake the custards, uncovered, for 1 hour or until set. Serve warm or cold.

LOW-FAT TIRAMISU

Now you can enjoy your favourite Italian dessert without stressing about your waistline

SERVES 6 | PREPARATION 20 MINUTES | COOKING NIL

- 375 ml (1½ cups) strong brewed coffee
- 2 tablespoons Frangelico liqueur (optional)
- 2 eggwhites
- 250 ml (1 cup) ready-made low-fat custard
- 350 g low-fat fresh ricotta
- ¼ cup icing sugar, sifted
- 250 g packet sponge finger (savoiardi) biscuits
- 2 tablespoons cocoa powder, sifted

Combine the coffee and liqueur (if using) in a shallow dish. Set aside to cool. Using an electric mixer, beat the eggwhites in a small bowl to soft peaks. In a separate bowl, use the electric mixer to beat the custard, ricotta and icing sugar until smooth and well combined. Fold in the eggwhites.

Dip half the biscuits, one at a time, into the coffee mixture. Arrange in a single layer over the base of a 6 cm deep, 18 cm square ceramic dish.

Spread half the ricotta mixture over the biscuits. Repeat with the remaining biscuits, coffee mixture and ricotta mixture. Cover and refrigerate for at least 6 hours, or overnight if time permits. Dust with cocoa before serving.

TIP *Frangelico is a hazelnut-flavoured liqueur. You could also replace it with Marsala or Kahlua.*

1323 kj
Fat 9.7 g
Saturated fat 5.4 g
Carbohydrates 44.0 g
Protein 12.9 g
Sugars 31.1 g
Fibre 0.7 g

PER SERVE

GOLDEN PINEAPPLE UPSIDE-DOWN CAKE

Pineapple gives this cake a golden glow, and helps it taste sensationally sweet.

SERVES 10 | PREPARATION 20 MINUTES + COOLING TIME | COOKING 30 MINUTES

melted butter, to grease
1 tablespoon brown sugar
½ pineapple, peeled, cored, halved lengthwise, cut into 5 mm slices
4 eggs, separated
⅓ cup brown sugar, extra
2 teaspoons finely grated lemon zest
½ cup low-fat yoghurt
½ cup polenta (cornmeal)
⅓ cup self-raising flour
⅓ cup almond meal

Preheat oven to 180°C or 160°C fan-forced. Brush a round 22-cm cake tin with melted butter to grease. Line the base and side with non-stick baking paper. Sprinkle the base with 2 teaspoons of the sugar.

711 kj
Fat 5.1 g
Saturated fat 1.2 g
Carbohydrates 24.2 g
Protein 6.1 g
Sugars 10.9 g
Fibre 1.5 g

PER SERVE

Arrange the pineapple, overlapping slightly, over the sugar. Sprinkle with the remaining 2 teaspoons sugar.

Using an electric beater, whisk the egg yolks, extra sugar and lemon zest in a large bowl until pale and thick. Stir in the yoghurt and polenta. Add the flour and almond meal and stir until just combined.

Using a clean electric beater, whisk the eggwhites in a clean, dry bowl until soft peaks form. Use a large metal spoon to gently fold half the eggwhites into the polenta mixture. Fold in the remaining egg white.

Pour the mixture into the prepared tin. Bake for 30 minutes or until a skewer inserted in the centre comes out clean. Set aside in the tin for 30 minutes to cool slightly. Turn out onto a serving plate and serve warm or at room temperature.

CHOCOLATE FUDGE CAKE

This cake is very moist and meringue-like. For a delicious dessert, try serving it with fresh berries.

SERVES 12 | PREPARATION 20 MINUTES | COOKING 45 MINUTES

- 60 g dark chocolate, finely chopped
- ¼ cup cocoa, plus extra for dusting
- ¼ cup boiling water
- 6 eggwhites
- ¾ cup caster sugar
- ½ cup plain flour, sifted

412 kj
Fat 1.9 g
Saturated fat 1.6 g
Carbohydrates 17.6 g
Protein 2.9 g
Sugars 15.8 g
Fibre 0.5 g

PER SERVE

Preheat the oven to 170°C. Line the base and sides of a 20-cm springform cake tin with baking paper.

Place the chocolate and cocoa in a small bowl. Pour on the boiling water and stir until the chocolate has melted and the mixture is smooth.

Using an electric mixer, beat the eggwhites until soft peaks form. Add the sugar, 1 tablespoon at a time, and continue beating until the sugar has completely dissolved and the meringue is thick and glossy. Add the chocolate mixture and mix to combine. Use a metal spoon to gently fold in the flour until just combined. Pour into the prepared tin and bake for 45 minutes, or until firm. Cool in the oven with the door ajar.

Remove the cake from the tin and serve in wedges dusted with cocoa.

LOW-FAT BERRY & MERINGUE ICE CREAM CAKE

Ice cream cake is a refreshing dessert for hot summer days.

SERVES 12 | PREPARATION 10 MINUTES + FREEZING TIME | COOKING NIL

2 litres low-fat vanilla ice cream

500 g fresh or frozen mixed berries

100 g packet (10) pavlova nests

Stand the ice cream at room temperature until slightly softened (about 10–15 minutes). Line a 26-cm springform cake tin with baking paper.

Place the softened ice cream into a large bowl and add the mixed berries. Add the meringue nests, one at a time, crushing gently in your hands. Stir until well combined.

Spoon the mixture into the prepared cake tin. Cover with plastic wrap and place in the freezer. Freeze for 6 hours, or overnight, if time permits, until firm. Turn out onto a serving plate. Serve immediately.

462 kj
Fat 2.1 g
Saturated fat 1.3 g
Carbohydrates 19.8 g
Protein 3.3 g
Sugars 19.7 g
Fibre 1.2 g

PER SERVE

MANDARIN & STRAWBERRY CRUMBLES

These little mandarin and strawberry desserts with crunchy muesli topping can be served as an after-dinner dessert or as a sweet idea for brunch.

SERVES 4 | PREPARATION 10 MINUTES | COOKING 15–20 MINUTES

¼ cup caster sugar

4 mandarins, peeled and segmented

250 g punnet strawberries, hulled, washed, dried and quartered

1 cup natural muesli

1 tablespoon honey

Preheat oven to 180°C or 160°C fan-forced. Put 60 ml (¼ cup) water and the sugar in a saucepan over low heat. Cook, stirring, for 3 minutes or until the sugar dissolves. Increase the heat to medium and bring to the boil. Add the mandarins and strawberries and cook, stirring occasionally, for 2 minutes or until heated through.

Spoon the mandarin mixture into four 125-ml (½-cup) ramekins or ovenproof dishes. Place the dishes on a baking tray.

Combine the muesli and honey in a bowl. Sprinkle the mandarin mixture with the muesli mixture. Bake for 10–15 minutes or until the muesli is toasted. Remove from the oven and serve immediately.

938 kj
Fat 2.7 g
Saturated fat 0.6 g
Carbohydrates 45.3 g
Protein 5.2 g
Sugars 34.5 g
Fibre 6.0 g

PER SERVE

APPLE & CINNAMON CLAFOUTIS

Clafoutis is a classic French pudding, great with berries and peaches, as well as with apple.

SERVES 4 | PREPARATION 10 MINUTES | COOKING 25 MINUTES

¼ cup caster sugar

¼ cup plain flour

2 eggs

250 ml (1 cup) reduced-fat milk

400 g tin pie apple

2 teaspoons ground cinnamon

2 teaspoons icing sugar, to serve

Preheat oven to 180°C or 160°C fan-forced. Lightly grease four 125-ml (½-cup) ovenproof ramekins.

Combine the caster sugar and flour in a bowl. Whisk together the eggs and milk. Pour the egg mixture into the flour mixture and whisk until smooth.

Divide the pie apple among the ramekins. Spoon the egg mixture over the apple and sprinkle with the cinnamon. Place the ramekins on a baking tray. Bake for 25 minutes or until set. Set aside for 5 minutes before serving, dusted with icing sugar.

851 kj
Fat 3.7 g
Saturated fat 1.4 g
Carbohydrates 35.7 g
Protein 6.9 g
Sugars 29.0 g
Fibre 2.5 g

PER SERVE

LIGHT CHOCOLATE MOUSSE

This light, fluffy mousse is a decadent-seeming light treat!

SERVES 6 | PREPARATION 15 MINUTES + COOLING AND SETTING TIME | COOKING NIL

- 125 ml (½ cup) boiling water
- 2 teaspoons powdered gelatine
- 1½ tablespoons cocoa powder, plus 2 teaspoons extra, for dusting
- 4 eggs, separated
- ⅓ cup caster sugar

Combine the boiling water and gelatine in a jug. Whisk with a fork until the gelatine has completely dissolved. Stir in 1½ tablespoons cocoa, then set aside to cool for 10 minutes.

Using an electric mixer, beat the eggwhites in a large bowl until soft peaks form. Add the sugar, 1 tablespoon at a time, beating until the meringue is thick and glossy. With the mixer on high speed, add the egg yolks, one at a time, beating well after each addition.

Slowly pour the gelatine mixture into the egg mixture (make sure the mixtures are both at the same temperature before you combine them), beating constantly until well combined. Spoon the mixture into 6 serving cups. Refrigerate for 4 hours or until set and chilled.

Dust with remaining 2 teaspoons cocoa before serving. This mousse is delicious served with almond bread.

TIP *When beating eggwhites, add a small pinch of cream of tartar. This helps to stabilise the egg, producing a light, fluffy mousse.*

619 kj
Fat 5.3 g
Saturated fat 1.8 g
Carbohydrates 17.6 g
Protein 8.1 g
Sugars 16.7 g
Fibre 0.2 g

PER SERVE

MANGO & STRAWBERRY ICE

Using frozen mango gives this icy dessert a lovely velvety texture. Alternatively, add 1 cup of ice to the blender and don't freeze the mango. This will increase the quantity by 1 cup.

SERVES 4 | PREPARATION 10 MINUTES + FREEZING TIME | COOKING NIL

2 mangoes, diced

250 g punnet strawberries, hulled

1 small banana, peeled

60 ml (¼ cup) apple juice

200 g tub reduced-fat passionfruit yoghurt

almond bread, to serve

Place the mango onto a lined baking tray. Cover and place in the freezer for 3 hours, or until frozen.

Process or blend the frozen mangoes, half the strawberries, banana, apple juice and yoghurt until combined. Pour into 4 glasses. Slice the remaining strawberries and place on top. Serve with almond bread.

TIP *Note that the nutrition analysis includes 2 small pieces of almond bread.*

761 kj
Fat 2.2 g
Saturated fat 0.4 g
Carbohydrates 35.3 g
Protein 5.1 g
Sugars 23.7 g
Fibre 3.8 g

PER SERVE

CHOC-CHIP OATMEAL COOKIES

These crunchy chocolate oatmeal cookies are low in fat, so munch away without the guilt.

MAKES 24 (1 PER SERVE) | PREPARATION 15 MINUTES | COOKING 20 MINUTES

1 egg
60 ml (¼ cup) macadamia nut oil
2 tablespoons ready-made apple sauce
½ cup brown sugar
1 teaspoon vanilla extract
1 cup plain flour
1 teaspoon baking powder
1 cup rolled oats
100 g good-quality dark chocolate, chopped

Preheat oven to 180°C or 160°C fan-forced. Line 2 baking trays with baking paper.

Using a fork, whisk the egg, oil, apple sauce, sugar and vanilla in a bowl until combined. Sift the flour and baking powder over the egg mixture. Add the oats and chocolate and stir gently to combine.

Place tablespoons of the mixture on the prepared trays, allowing room for spreading. Bake for 15–20 minutes or until light golden. Leave the cookies on the trays for 5 minutes, then transfer to a wire rack to cool.

400 kj
Fat 4.2 g
Saturated fat 1.6 g
Carbohydrates 12.6 g
Protein 1.1 g
Sugars 6.0 g
Fibre 0.8 g

PER SERVE

MANGO SORBET

This is a great way to enjoy mango when it's in season.

SERVES 6 | PREPARATION 15 MINUTES + FREEZING TIME | COOKING NIL

250 ml (1 cup) fresh orange juice

60 ml (¼ cup) fresh lemon juice

¼ cup sugar

3 medium mangoes, peeled, flesh sliced

Put the orange juice, lemon juice and sugar into a medium saucepan and bring to the boil over medium heat. Reduce the heat to low and simmer for 3 minutes. Set aside to cool.

Place the mango flesh and cooled orange syrup into the bowl of a food processor or blender and process until smooth. Pour the mango mixture into a metal or plastic container, then cover and freeze for 2 hours or until almost set.

Remove the mango sorbet from the freezer and roughly break up with a metal spoon. Transfer to the bowl of a food processor and process very briefly until it has a smooth, soft icy texture. Transfer the sorbet back into the container and freeze for a further 2–3 hours or until firm.

Transfer the sorbet to the fridge 10 minutes before serving to soften slightly. Scoop into glasses or dishes and serve immediately. Serve with almond bread if desired.

461 kj
Fat 0.2 g
Saturated fat 0.0 g
Carbohydrates 25.6 g
Protein 1.3 g
Sugars 0.5 g
Fibre 1.6 g

PER SERVE

MIXED BERRY CHEESECAKE BROWNIES

All our favourite desserts unite to create the ultimate taste sensation!

MAKES 24 (1 PER SERVE) | PREPARATION 15 MINUTES | COOKING 1 HOUR

melted butter, to grease
100 g good-quality dark chocolate, chopped
125 ml (½ cup) warm water
60 g reduced-fat dairy spread
¾ cup firmly packed brown sugar
2 eggs, lightly whisked
½ cup plain flour
⅓ cup self-raising flour
½ cup cocoa powder
250 g packet light cream cheese
1 cup low-fat ricotta
¼ cup caster sugar
1 egg, extra, lightly whisked
300 g frozen mixed berries

589 kj
Fat 6.4 g
Saturated fat 3.9 g
Carbohydrates 16.7 g
Protein 4.0 g
Sugars 12.4 g
Fibre 1.0 g

PER SERVE

Preheat oven to 180°C or 160°C fan-forced. Brush a 20 cm x 30 cm cake tin with melted butter to lightly grease.

Combine the chocolate, warm water and dairy spread in a saucepan over low heat. Cook, stirring, for 5 minutes or until the chocolate melts and the mixture is smooth. Remove from the heat. Add the brown sugar and stir to combine. Set aside for 5 minutes to cool.

Add the egg, combined flours and cocoa powder and stir to combine. Spoon the mixture into the prepared tin and smooth the surface.

Use an electric beater to beat the cream cheese, ricotta, caster sugar and extra egg in a bowl until smooth. Stir in half the berries. Pour the cream cheese mixture over the chocolate mixture and sprinkle with the remaining berries.

Bake for 50–60 minutes or until the topping is set. Remove from the oven. Set aside for 30 minutes to cool, then place in the fridge to cool completely. Cut into 24 pieces to serve.

CINNAMON RICOTTA BAKED PEACHES

The combination of ricotta, cinnamon and peaches is divine!

SERVES 4 | PREPARATION 15 MINUTES | COOKING 10 MINUTES

4 large, ripe freestone peaches
200 g ricotta
1 tablespoon icing sugar mixture
½ teaspoon ground cinnamon
1 tablespoon honey
12 slices almond bread, to serve

Preheat oven to 200°C or 180°C fan-forced. Cut a small cross in the base of each peach. Place in a heatproof bowl and cover with boiling water. Set aside for 2 minutes. Using a slotted spoon, transfer the peaches to a board (draining will bruise the peaches). Peel and discard skin. Cut the peaches in half and remove the stones. Place the peaches in a single layer, cut side up, in a baking dish.

Using an electric mixer, beat the ricotta, icing sugar and cinnamon in a bowl until smooth. Spoon the ricotta mixture into the cavity of each peach. Bake for 8–10 minutes or until light golden.

Place the peaches on serving plates and drizzle with honey. Serve warm with almond bread.

1030 kj
Fat 7.4 g
Saturated fat 4.0 g
Carbohydrates 34.0 g
Protein 9.0 g
Sugars 25.9 g
Fibre 3.4 g

PER SERVE

BERRY & HONEY SEMIFREDDO

Raspberries, strawberries, yoghurt and honey – what could be better?

SERVES 8 | PREPARATION 15 MINUTES + FREEZING TIME | COOKING NIL

- 3 eggs
- ¼ cup honey
- 2 cups low-fat vanilla yoghurt
- 190 g raspberries
- 250 g punnet strawberries, hulled and halved
- 2 teaspoons icing sugar mixture, sifted

Use an electric beater to beat the eggs and honey together for 5 minutes or until pale and creamy. Stir in the yoghurt.

Line the base and 2 long sides of a 1.5-litre (6-cup) loaf tin with plastic wrap, allowing the sides to overhang. Pour in the egg mixture and fold over the plastic wrap to cover. Place in the freezer for 2 hours or until almost set.

Use a fork to mash 125 g (1 cup) raspberries in a bowl. Swirl the mashed raspberry through the semifreddo. Cover and freeze overnight.

Transfer the semifreddo to the fridge 20 minutes before serving to soften slightly. Combine the strawberries, icing sugar and remaining raspberries in a bowl. Turn the semifreddo out onto a plate and remove the plastic wrap. Cut into slices and serve with the mixed berries.

553 kj
Fat 2.2 g
Saturated fat 0.6 g
Carbohydrates 19.7 g
Protein 7.1 g
Sugars 19.6 g
Fibre 2.0 g

PER SERVE

MELON & STARFRUIT IN KAFFIR LIME SYRUP

Ginger, kaffir lime and exotic fruits mingle with delicious results in this delightful fruit dessert.

SERVES 4 | PREPARATION 10 MINUTES + COOLING TIME | COOKING 10 MINUTES

¼ cup caster sugar

2 x 5 mm thick slices ginger

4 kaffir lime leaves, bruised

1 tablespoon lime juice

¼ rockmelon, seeded and chopped

2 starfruit, sliced

2 slices of watermelon, rind removed, cut into wedges

mango sorbet, to serve

Put the sugar, ginger and 125 ml (½ cup) water in a saucepan over medium-high heat and stir until the sugar dissolves. Bring to the boil, then reduce the heat to medium and simmer for 7–10 minutes or until the syrup thickens slightly.

Add the lime leaves and set aside to cool. When the syrup is cool, remove the lime leaves and ginger. Stir in the lime juice.

Divide the fruit among serving bowls. Pour over the syrup and serve with sorbet.

729 kj
Fat 0.4 g
Saturated fat 0.0 g
Carbohydrates 42.4 g
Protein 1.4 g
Sugars 42.2 g
Fibre 2.0 g

PER SERVE

PINEAPPLE & GINGER UPSIDE-DOWN CAKE

Enjoy this classic upside-down cake with a low-cal twist.

SERVES 8 | PREPARATION 15 MINUTES | COOKING 45 MINUTES

- melted reduced-fat dairy spread, to grease
- ⅓ cup firmly packed brown sugar, plus ½ cup extra
- ½ ripe pineapple, peeled and cored, cut crosswise into 3 mm thick slices
- ¼ cup finely chopped sucrose-free glacé ginger (Buderim Ginger brand)
- 3 eggs
- 140 g apple fruit purée
- 3 tablespoons reduced-fat dairy spread, melted and cooled
- 1¾ cups self-raising flour
- 2 teaspoons ground ginger
- 60 ml (¼ cup) reduced-fat milk

1232 kj
Fat 6.5 g
Saturated fat 2.5 g
Carbohydrates 52.6 g
Protein 6.8 g
Sugars 28.1 g
Fibre 2.6 g

PER SERVE

Preheat oven to 180°C or 160°C fan-forced. Brush a round 22-cm cake tin with melted dairy spread to lightly grease.

Sprinkle the brown sugar evenly over the base of the prepared tin. Arrange the pineapple slices, overlapping slightly, over the brown sugar to cover the base of the tin. Sprinkle evenly with the glacé ginger.

Place the eggs, extra brown sugar, apple purée and melted dairy spread in a large bowl. Use a wire balloon whisk to whisk until well combined. Sift over the flour and ground ginger. Use a metal spoon to fold the egg mixture, flour mixture and milk together until well combined. Pour the mixture over the pineapple in the tin and smooth the surface.

Bake for 45 minutes or until a skewer inserted into the centre of the cake comes out clean. Remove from the oven. Set aside in the tin for 10 minutes. Carefully turn out onto a serving platter or cake stand. Serve warm or at room temperature.

GLAZED VANILLA PLUMS

Yoghurt is a great accompaniment to these sweet glazed plums.

SERVES 4 | PREPARATION 10 MINUTES | COOKING 10 MINUTES

¼ cup flaked almonds

2 tablespoons brown sugar

6 blood plums, halved and stones removed

½ teaspoon vanilla extract

½ cup low-fat vanilla yoghurt

Heat a non-stick frying pan over medium heat. Add the almonds and cook, stirring often, for 2–3 minutes or until light golden. Transfer to a plate and set aside.

Reduce the heat to low. Add the sugar and 60 ml (¼ cup) cold water to the frying pan. Cook, stirring, for 2 minutes or until the sugar dissolves. Bring to a simmer and cook for a further 2–3 minutes or until the sauce reduces and is syrupy. Add the plums. Cook, carefully turning the plums occasionally, for 3 minutes or until the plums are heated through and glazed. Stir in the vanilla.

Spoon the plums and syrup into bowls. Sprinkle with the toasted almonds and serve warm or cold with yoghurt.

TIP *You could use tinned plums in juice instead of fresh. Drain the plums and pat dry with paper towel before adding them to the syrup.*

536 kj
Fat 3.8 g
Saturated fat 0.6 g
Carbohydrates 18.8 g
Protein 18.8 g
Sugars 18.2 g
Fibre 2.6 g

PER SERVE

PINK LADIES WITH FRUIT & NUT CHEESE

This is a great way to enjoy your apple a day!

SERVES 4 | PREPARATION 10 MINUTES | COOKING NIL

- 4 pink lady apples, cut into wedges, core removed
- finely grated zest and juice of 1 lemon
- 250 g cream cheese, at room temperature
- 40 g dried peach, finely diced
- 20 g walnuts, chopped
- 20 g pistachio kernels, chopped
- 20 g dark chocolate, finely chopped

Place the apple wedges in a bowl and squeeze over the lemon juice.

Use a wooden spoon to beat the cream cheese until smooth. Add the lemon zest, dried peach, walnuts, pistachios and chocolate. Mix until well combined. Serve with the apple wedges.

1775 kj
Fat 28.5 g
Saturated fat 15.1 g
Carbohydrates 35.4 g
Protein 8.4 g
Sugars 33.7 g
Fibre 6.0 g

PER SERVE

RICOTTA & RASPBERRY CHEESECAKES

Using ricotta and tofu is a great way to enjoy cheesecake but not break the diet.

SERVES 6 | PREPARATION 10 MINUTES + CHILLING TIME | COOKING 40 MINUTES

200 g fresh ricotta

300 g silken tofu, drained well

½ cup caster sugar

finely grated zest and juice of 1 lime

2 eggs

300 g frozen raspberries, thawed on paper towel

icing sugar, to dust

Preheat oven to 160°C or 140°C fan-forced. Lightly grease six 125-ml (½-cup) ramekins or ovenproof dishes.

Use an electric beater to beat the ricotta, tofu, sugar and lime zest until well combined and almost smooth. Beat in the lime juice and eggs. Stir in the raspberries, reserving a few for garnish.

Spoon the ricotta mixture into the ramekins and smooth the surface. Place the ramekins in a baking dish and pour in enough hot water to reach halfway up the sides of the ramekins. Bake for 40 minutes or until just firm. Set aside in the water bath for 10 minutes.

Remove the ramekins from the water and set aside to cool to room temperature, then cover and place in the fridge for 3–4 hours or until well chilled. Garnish with the reserved raspberries and dust with icing sugar.

829 kj
Fat 6.6 g
Saturated fat 3.1 g
Carbohydrates 24.6 g
Protein 10.0 g
Sugars 23.5 g
Fibre 4.1 g

PER SERVE

JELLIED BERRIES

Berries are full of antioxidants, and so good for you!

SERVES 4 | PREPARATION 10 MINUTES | COOKING NIL

- 9 g sachet low-kilojoule raspberry jelly crystals
- 250 ml (1 cup) boiling water
- 250 g strawberries, hulled and sliced
- 150 g blueberries
- 375 ml (1½ cups) low-fat vanilla custard

Place the jelly crystals in a jug. Pour over boiling water and stir until completely dissolved. Stir in 250 ml (1 cup) cold water.

Pour the jelly into four 250-ml (1-cup) glasses. Spoon half the strawberries and blueberries into the jellies. Cover and refrigerate for at least 4 hours or until set.

Top the jellies with the remaining strawberries and blueberries. Serve with the custard.

464 kj
Fat 1.1 g
Saturated fat 0.6 g
Carbohydrates 19.7 g
Protein 4.9 g
Sugars 16.4 g
Fibre 2.1 g
PER SERVE

PIKELETTAS WITH STRAWBERRY RICOTTA CREAM

The strawberry ricotta cream is a to-die-for element of this dessert.

MAKES 20 (1 PER SERVE) | PREPARATION 35 MINUTES + 20 MINUTES RESTING | COOKING 10 MINUTES

¼ cup self-raising flour
1 tablespoon caster sugar
small pinch of bicarbonate of soda
1 eggwhite, lightly whisked
2 tablespoons reduced-fat milk
4 strawberries, cut into sixths lengthwise

Strawberry ricotta cream
100 g reduced-fat fresh ricotta
2 tablespoons pure icing sugar, sifted
75 g strawberries, finely diced

Sift the flour, sugar and bicarbonate of soda into a small bowl. Make a well in the centre. Whisk the eggwhite and milk together in a jug. Use a wooden spoon to gradually mix the milk mixture into the flour mixture to make a smooth batter. Cover with plastic wrap and set aside for 20 minutes to rest.

Heat a non-stick frying pan over medium heat. Drop 1 teaspoon of batter into the pan from the tip of the spoon for each pikeletta, allowing room for spreading. Cook for 1 minute or until golden underneath and bubbles appear on the surface. Use a spatula to turn the pikelettas and cook for 30 seconds or until golden underneath. Transfer to a wire rack to cool. Repeat with the remaining batter.

To make the strawberry ricotta cream, mix the ricotta and icing sugar with a wooden spoon until well combined. Fold in the diced strawberries.

Just before serving, place 1 teaspoon of the strawberry ricotta cream on each pikeletta and top with a piece of strawberry. Serve immediately.

TIP *You can make the pikelettas up to 6 hours ahead. Store in an airtight container. Make the strawberry ricotta cream up to 2 hours ahead. Store in an airtight container in the fridge.*

102 kj
Fat 0.5 g
Saturated fat 0.3 g
Carbohydrates 3.8 g
Protein 1.1 g
Sugars 2.4 g
Fibre 0.3 g
PER SERVE

WATERMELON, PEACH & STRAWBERRY GRANITA

This fruity granita is a refreshing treat.

SERVES 6 | PREPARATION 10 MINUTES + FREEZING TIME | COOKING NIL

- 1 kg seedless watermelon, skin removed, chopped
- 2 x 250 g punnets strawberries, hulled and sliced
- 425 g tin peach slices in natural juice
- 2 tablespoons caster sugar

Place the watermelon, strawberries, peach slices and peach juice into a food processor (in batches if necessary) and process until smooth. Add sugar to taste.

Pour the fruit mixture through a sieve into a shallow 2-litre (8-cup) plastic container. Cover and freeze for 4–5 hours or until partially set. Use a fork to flake the granita to break it up, then cover and freeze for a further 4 hours or until completely frozen. Use a fork to flake the granita again and break up the ice crystals. Return to the freezer until ready to serve.

Spoon the granita into chilled serving glasses and serve immediately.

TIP *As a variation, you could replace the strawberries with raspberries (fresh or frozen) and the peaches with tinned mango slices.*

500 kj
Fat 0.5 g
Saturated fat 0.0 g
Carbohydrates 23.8 g
Protein 3.0 g
Sugars 23.0 g
Fibre 3.6 g

PER SERVE

BAKED APPLES WITH FRUIT MINCE

Baked apples are a traditional favourite that are always in fashion.

SERVES 4 | PREPARATION 10 MINUTES | COOKING 30 MINUTES

- 4 small Granny Smith apples
- 1½ tablespoons fruit mince
- 125 ml (½ cup) apple and mango juice
- 125 ml (½ cup) low-fat vanilla custard, to serve

Preheat oven to 180°C or 160°C fan-forced. Using an apple corer, core the apples. Slice around the middle of each apple skin to prevent bursting during cooking.

Place the apples in a ceramic baking dish. Spoon the fruit mince into the apple centres, then pour over the juice. Bake for 25–30 minutes, basting every 10 minutes with juice, or until the apples are just tender.

Divide the apples among serving plates. Spoon over the juice and serve with custard.

TIP *To prevent apples 'exploding' during baking, use a sharp knife to cut a 5 mm deep circle around the top, middle and base of each apple. This also allows heat to penetrate the fruit, reducing the cooking time.*

464 kj
Fat 0.7 g
Saturated fat 0.3 g
Carbohydrates 24.3 g
Protein 1.6 g
Sugars 22.6 g
Fibre 2.2 g

PER SERVE

LEMON & PISTACHIO PUDDINGS

Lemon and pistachio are a delicious combination in these mouth-watering puddings.

SERVES 4 | PREPARATION 20 MINUTES | COOKING 10–15 MINUTES

- 2 tablespoons pistachio kernels
- 2 eggs, separated
- 2 tablespoons caster sugar
- finely grated zest and juice of 1 lemon
- 1 tablespoon plain flour
- 1 tablespoon skim milk
- 2 teaspoons pure icing sugar

Preheat oven to 180°C or 160°C fan-forced. Grease four 150-ml ramekins. Set aside 12 pistachio kernels. Finely chop the remaining pistachios.

Using electric beaters, beat the egg yolks and caster sugar together for 3 minutes or until pale and creamy. Add the lemon zest, flour, milk, chopped pistachios and 2 tablespoons of lemon juice. Beat on low speed until just combined.

Wash and dry the beaters. Beat the eggwhites in a bowl until soft peaks form. Fold the eggwhites into the lemon mixture until well combined. Spoon the mixture into the prepared ramekins until three-quarters full. Place on a baking tray. Bake for 10–15 minutes or until set in the centre.

Roughly chop the reserved pistachios and sprinkle over the puddings. Dust with icing sugar and serve.

587 kj
Fat 7.0 g
Saturated fat 1.3 g
Carbohydrates 13.7 g
Protein 5.4 g
Sugars 10.7 g
Fibre 0.9 g

PER SERVE

PUMPKIN CUSTARD PIE

This delicious pumpkin custard pie is an unusual treat!

SERVES 6 | PREPARATION 20 MINUTES | COOKING 1 HOUR 30 MINUTES

melted butter, to grease

850 g jap pumpkin, unpeeled, seeded, cut into chunks

3 eggs, lightly whisked

2 eggwhites, extra, lightly whisked

⅓ cup pure maple syrup

⅓ cup reduced-fat milk

1 tablespoon plain flour

½ teaspoon ground cardamom

pinch of ground cinnamon

200 g light vanilla Frûche, to serve

825 kj
Fat 5.3 g
Saturated fat 2.6 g
Carbohydrates 27.2 g
Protein 9.8 g
Sugars 22.8 g
Fibre 1.8 g

PER SERVE

Preheat oven to 180°C or 160°C fan-forced. Brush a round 24-cm fluted quiche or pie dish with the melted butter to lightly grease.

Place the pumpkin on a baking tray and roast for 45 minutes or until tender. Set aside for 30 minutes to cool.

Peel the pumpkin and place in the bowl of a food processor. Process, scraping down the side of the bowl often, until the pumpkin is smooth. Add the eggs, eggwhites, maple syrup, milk, flour, cardamom and cinnamon and process until the mixture is well combined.

Pour the mixture into the greased dish and bake for 45 minutes or until the centre is firm. Set aside for 30 minutes to cool slightly. Cut into wedges and serve with a dollop of Frûche. Store the pie in an airtight container in the fridge for up to 2 days.

APRICOT FRUIT BARS

Enjoy these snacks with none of the guilt – they taste delicious but are low carb and low fat.

SERVES 6 | PREPARATION 20 MINUTES + RESTING AND CHILLING TIME | COOKING 5 MINUTES

1 cup chopped dried apricots

¾ cup raisins

½ cup chopped pitted prunes

125 ml (½ cup) fresh orange juice

1 cup skim milk powder

½ cup fresh wholemeal breadcrumbs

½ cup slivered almonds

½ cup sunflower seed kernels

Combine the apricots, raisins, prunes and orange juice in a saucepan. Bring to the boil, then remove from the heat, cover and set aside for 15 minutes.

Add the milk powder, breadcrumbs and almonds and mix well. Sprinkle half the sunflower seeds over the base of a non-stick 18 cm x 28 cm shallow tin.

Press the apricot mixture firmly into the tin and sprinkle with the remaining sunflower seeds, pressing them into the mixture. Cover and place in the fridge for 2–4 hours or until firm. Cut into bars to serve.

367 kj
Fat 3.1 g
Saturated fat 0.2 g
Carbohydrates 10.9 g
Protein 3.3 g
Sugars 9.6 g
Fibre 1.7 g

PER SERVE

LIME & WATERMELON SORBET

Sorbet is a great low-fat alternative to ice cream.

SERVES 4 | PREPARATION 15 MINUTES + FREEZING TIME | COOKING 15 MINUTES

½ cup caster sugar
250 ml (1 cup) warm water
750 g peeled watermelon, chopped
1 teaspoon finely grated lime zest
60 ml (¼ cup) lime juice
2 eggwhites, lightly whisked

Combine the sugar and warm water in a saucepan over medium heat. Cook, stirring, for 5 minutes or until the sugar dissolves. Simmer without stirring for 10 minutes or until the mixture thickens slightly. Remove from the heat and set aside to cool completely.

Place the watermelon in a food processor or blender and process until smooth. Using a fine sieve, strain the watermelon into a large bowl. Discard the pulp. Add the sugar mixture, lime zest and lime juice to the bowl, and stir to combine. Pour into a 3-cm deep, 20 cm x 30 cm cake tin. Cover and freeze for 1–2 hours or until almost firm.

Transfer the partially frozen watermelon mixture to a food processor. Add the eggwhites and process until the mixture is smooth but not melted. Pour the mixture into a 6-cm deep, 12 cm x 22 cm loaf tin. Cover and freeze for 3 hours or until firm.

600 kj
Fat 0.4 g
Saturated fat 0.0 g
Carbohydrates 36.1 g
Protein 2.4 g
Sugars 36.1 g
Fibre 1.1 g

PER SERVE

HONEY, SULTANA & BRAN SLICE

This is a healthy slice for afternoon tea.

MAKES 24 (1 PER SERVE) | PREPARATION 15 MINUTES | COOKING 30 MINUTES

melted butter, to grease
1½ cups wholemeal self-raising flour
1¼ cups sultanas
2 cups bran flakes
¾ cup honey
60 ml (¼ cup) vegetable oil
2 eggs, lightly whisked
1 teaspoon ground nutmeg
1 tablespoon sesame seeds

Preheat oven to 180°C or 160°C fan-forced. Brush a 20 cm x 30 cm cake tin with the melted butter to lightly grease. Line the base with non-stick baking paper.

Place the flour, sultanas and bran flakes in a food processor. Process in short bursts until the sultanas are roughly chopped.

Put the honey, oil, eggs and nutmeg in a bowl and mix well. Add the flour mixture and use a wooden spoon to stir until well combined. Spoon the mixture into the lined tin and spread evenly over the base. Sprinkle evenly with the sesame seeds.

Bake for 30 minutes or until cooked through. Cool the slice in the tin before removing and cutting into pieces. Store the slice in an airtight container for up to 5 days.

605 kj
Fat 3.7 g
Saturated fat 0.7 g
Carbohydrates 24.9 g
Protein 2.5 g
Sugars 16.8 g
Fibre 2.0 g

PER SERVE

SEMOLINA PUDDING WITH CURRANTS

Currants, toasted almonds, spices and vanilla mingle in this delicious pudding.

SERVES 6 | PREPARATION 10 MINUTES + COOLING TIME | COOKING 15 MINUTES

- ¼ cup flaked almonds
- 3 teaspoons butter
- ⅓ cup semolina
- 1.185 litres (4¾ cups) reduced-fat milk
- ⅓ cup caster sugar
- ½ vanilla bean, split lengthwise
- 1 teaspoon ground cardamom
- 2½ tablespoons currants
- ¼ teaspoon ground nutmeg
- 1 tablespoon sultanas

Preheat oven to 180°C or 160°C fan-forced. Spread the almonds over a baking tray and toast in the oven for 5–7 minutes or until golden. Transfer to a bowl and set aside.

Melt the butter in a large saucepan over medium heat. Add the semolina and cook, stirring, for 4–5 minutes or until light golden. Transfer to a heatproof bowl.

Combine the milk and sugar in the pan. Use a small sharp knife to scrape the seeds from the vanilla bean into the milk mixture. Stir in the cardamom. Bring to the boil over medium–high heat, then add the semolina and return to the boil, stirring constantly. Cook, uncovered, stirring, for 2–3 minutes or until the mixture thickens. Stir in 2 tablespoons each of almonds and currants.

Spoon the semolina into heatproof serving bowls and set aside for 30 minutes to cool. Serve sprinkled with the nutmeg, remaining almonds and currants, and sultanas.

1182 kj
Fat 7.1 g
Saturated fat 3.2 g
Carbohydrates 43.6 g
Protein 11.2 g
Sugars 29.1 g
Fibre 1.4 g

PER SERVE

MANGO & YOGHURT POPS

These pops are delicious and refreshing summer treats.

SERVES 8 | PREPARATION 10 MINUTES + FREEZING TIME | COOKING NIL

3 ripe mangoes, cheeks removed, coarsely chopped

1 cup vanilla yoghurt

Place the mango flesh in the bowl of a food processor and process until smooth. Transfer to a bowl. Add the yoghurt and gently fold until the mixture is just combined. Spoon the mango mixture evenly among eight 80-ml (¾-cup) ice-block moulds. Place in the freezer for 8 hours or until firm.

TIP *Try making berry pops, too. Simply replace the mango with strawberries and use berry yoghurt instead of the vanilla yoghurt.*

259 kj
Fat 0.8 g
Saturated fat 0.4 g
Carbohydrates 10.6 g
Protein 2.2 g
Sugars 10.2 g
Fibre 1.0 g

PER SERVE

STRAWBERRY JAM PUDDINGS

These delicious puddings are strawberry-flavoured delights!

SERVES 6 | PREPARATION 15 MINUTES | COOKING 15 MINUTES

½ cup diet strawberry conserve (or use apricot or raspberry)

¼ cup reduced-fat dairy spread

¼ cup caster sugar

1 teaspoon vanilla essence

1 egg

½ cup self-raising flour

¼ cup almond meal

1 tablespoon skim milk

Preheat oven to 170°C or 150°C fan-forced. Lightly grease six 125-ml (½-cup) ovenproof dishes. Spread 1 tablespoon of conserve over the base of each dish.

Using an electric mixer, beat the spread, sugar and vanilla until pale and creamy. Add the egg and beat until well combined. Sift the flour and almond meal together into a bowl. Add half the flour mixture to the egg mixture. Mix well, then add the remaining flour mixture and the milk. Stir gently to combine.

Spoon the batter over the conserve, and smooth the surface. Bake for 15 minutes or until a skewer inserted into the centre of the batter comes out clean. Serve in the dishes or alternatively, use a knife to loosen the edges of the puddings. Turn out onto serving plates.

TIP *For chocolate puddings, replace the jam with Nutella, add 2 tablespoons cocoa powder with the flour and increase the milk to 2 tablespoons.*

894 kj
Fat 9.5 g
Saturated fat 4.3 g
Carbohydrates 29.0 g
Protein 3.5 g
Sugars 20.8 g
Fibre 1.5 g

PER SERVE

CINNAMON, CHERRY & PEAR MUFFINS

This unusual combination of flavours makes for intriguing muffins.

MAKES 4 (1 PER SERVE) | PREPARATION 15 MINUTES | COOKING 25 MINUTES

1 cup self-raising flour, sifted

½ teaspoon ground cinnamon

2 tablespoons caster sugar

50 g reduced-fat canola spread, melted and cooled

80 ml (⅓ cup) skim milk

1 egg

½ cup tinned seedless black cherries, drained and halved

½ cup tinned pears, drained and chopped

pure icing sugar, to serve

Preheat oven to 200°C or 180°C fan-forced. Lightly grease four 185-ml (¾-cup) Texas muffin holes.

Combine the flour, cinnamon and sugar in a bowl. Make a well in the centre. Whisk together the melted spread, milk and egg in a jug, and pour into the well. Add the cherries and pears. Stir gently using a large metal spoon until just combined (do not overmix).

Three-quarter fill each muffin hole with the mixture. Bake for 20–25 minutes or until a skewer inserted into the centre of a muffin comes out clean. Stand the muffins in the tin for 4 minutes. Turn out onto a wire rack to cool slightly. Dust with icing sugar and serve warm.

1153 kj
Fat 8.7 g
Saturated fat 3.5 g
Carbohydrates 42.2 g
Protein 6.4 g
Sugars 17.1 g
Fibre 2.1 g

PER SERVE

BANANA & COCONUT SEMIFREDDO

Finish your low-fat feast off with this tasty frozen dessert.

SERVES 6 | PREPARATION 10 MINUTES + FREEZING TIME | COOKING NIL

- 2 small bananas, peeled and chopped
- ¾ cup low-fat vanilla yoghurt
- 200 ml low-fat evaporated milk
- 100 ml pineapple juice
- ½ teaspoon coconut essence
- ¼ teaspoon ground nutmeg
- 250 g punnet strawberries, hulled and sliced

Place the bananas, yoghurt, evaporated milk, pineapple juice, coconut essence and nutmeg in a blender. Blend until smooth.

Pour into a 1-litre (4-cup) airtight container. Freeze for 4–5 hours or until just frozen. Spoon into bowls and serve with strawberries.

TIP *The semifreddo will keep in the freezer for up to 1 month. Before serving, you might need to let it stand in the fridge for 15 minutes to soften slightly before scooping.*

400 kj
Fat 1.4 g
Saturated fat 0.8 g
Carbohydrates 14.5 g
Protein 5.5 g
Sugars 13.6 g
Fibre 1.5 g

PER SERVE

PEAR & RHUBARB COMPOTE

Compotes are healthy and delicious dessert options.

SERVES 4 | PREPARATION 15 MINUTES | COOKING 40 MINUTES

- 3 ripe pears, peeled, cored and cut into thick wedges
- 1 bunch rhubarb, ends trimmed, cut into 6 cm lengths
- 60 ml (¼ cup) fresh orange juice
- 1 vanilla bean, split lengthways
- 1 cinnamon stick
- 2 tablespoons raw (demerara) sugar
- 250 ml (1 cup) low-fat custard, to serve

Preheat oven to 180°C or 160°C fan-forced. Arrange the pears and rhubarb in a shallow ovenproof dish and pour over the orange juice.

Add the vanilla bean and cinnamon stick and stir gently to combine. Sprinkle over the sugar. Cover with foil and bake for 40 minutes or until the fruit is tender.

Spoon the compote into bowls and serve immediately with custard.

884 kj
Fat 1.5 g
Saturated fat 0.6 g
Carbohydrates 41.5 g
Protein 6.9 g
Sugars 34.3 g
Fibre 13.2 g

PER SERVE

CARROT & SUNFLOWER SEED MUFFINS WITH LEMON ICING

Bite into these gluten-free carrot muffins, which are low in fat but packed with flavour.

MAKES 12 (1 PER SERVE) | PREPARATION 20 MINUTES | COOKING 20 MINUTES

3 eggs

140 g container apple fruit purée

125 ml (½ cup) reduced-fat milk or light soy milk

⅓ cup brown sugar

1 tablespoon light olive oil

1¼ cups firmly packed finely shredded carrot

2 tablespoons sunflower seed kernels, plus 1½ tablespoons extra

1 teaspoon finely grated lemon zest

1¾ cups gluten-free all-purpose flour mix

3½ teaspoons gluten-free baking powder

½ teaspoon mixed spice

Lemon icing

1 cup pure icing sugar

2 teaspoons finely grated lemon zest

1 teaspoon melted butter

1–2 tablespoons lemon juice

915 kj
Fat 5.3 g
Saturated fat 0.9 g
Carbohydrates 39.8 g
Protein 2.7 g
Sugars 20.9 g
Fibre 1.3 g
PER SERVE

Preheat oven to 180°C or 160°C fan-forced. Line a 12-hole 80-ml (⅓-cup) muffin tray with paper cases.

Whisk together the eggs, apple purée, milk, brown sugar and oil in a large bowl until well combined. Stir in the carrot, sunflower seeds and lemon zest.

Sift the flour mix, baking powder and mixed spice into the carrot mixture. Use a large metal spoon to fold until well combined. Spoon the batter evenly into the muffin cases.

Bake for 18–20 minutes or until a skewer inserted into the centre of a muffin comes out clean. Remove from the oven. Turn the muffins out onto a wire rack and set aside to cool completely.

Meanwhile, to make the lemon icing, sift the icing sugar into a bowl. Add the lemon zest and melted butter. Stir in the lemon juice until a smooth paste forms. Drizzle the muffins with icing and sprinkle with the extra sunflower seeds. Set aside for 15 minutes to set.

LIGHT BAKED LEMON CHEESECAKE

Baked cheesecakes don't have to be off the menu when you're watching your waistline!

SERVES 8 | PREPARATION 15 MINUTES + COOLING AND CHILLING TIME | COOKING 1 HOUR

melted butter, to grease

70 g (about 4) sponge finger (savoiardi) biscuits, finely chopped

750 g fresh reduced-fat ricotta

¾ cup caster sugar

3 eggs, lightly whisked

finely grated zest and juice of 1 large lemon

icing sugar, to dust

Preheat oven to 150°C or 130°C fan-forced. Brush a 20-cm springform tin with the melted butter to lightly grease. Line the base and side with non-stick baking paper and spread the sponge finger biscuits evenly over the base of the tin.

Use electric beaters to whisk the ricotta and sugar until well combined. Add the eggs a little at a time, whisking well after each addition. Add the lemon zest and 60 ml (¼ cup) lemon juice, and whisk well to combine.

Carefully pour the filling evenly over the biscuits in the tin. Lightly tap the tin on the bench to settle the mixture. Bake for 1 hour or until the centre of the cheesecake trembles slightly when the side of the tin is gently tapped. Turn the oven off and place a wooden spoon inside the door to hold it slightly ajar so the cheesecake cools slowly. This will take 2–3 hours.

Tightly wrap the cooled cheesecake (still in the tin) in plastic wrap and then foil, and place in the fridge overnight to chill before serving.

To serve, remove the cheesecake from the tin and dust with icing sugar. Use a thin-bladed knife to cut into wedges, dipping the knife in warm water and wiping dry between each cut.

1013 kj
Fat 11.3 g
Saturated fat 6.7 g
Carbohydrates 23.3 g
Protein 12.6 g
Sugars 21.0 g
Fibre 0.4 g

PER SERVE

STRAWBERRY TRIFLES

Whip up dessert in a flash with these deliciously low-fat strawberry trifles.

SERVES 4 | PREPARATION 15 MINUTES + CHILLING TIME | COOKING NIL

2 tablespoons apple juice

1 teaspoon vanilla extract

2 x 250 g punnets strawberries, hulled and sliced

12 sponge finger biscuits, cut in half

170 ml (⅓ cup) low-fat custard

Put the apple juice, vanilla and half the strawberries in a food processor or blender and process until smooth.

Place the biscuits in a bowl. Working quickly, pour the strawberry mixture over the biscuits and stir until just coated.

Spoon 2 heaped tablespoons of biscuit mixture into the base of four 250-ml (1-cup) dishes or glasses. Top each with 1 tablespoon custard. Arrange 3 or 4 strawberry slices over the custard. Repeat the layers twice. Cover and refrigerate for 30 minutes before serving.

TIP *When storing strawberries, remove the strawberries from the punnet and place in a single layer on a plate or in an airtight container. Cover and refrigerate for up to 3 days. Wash the strawberries in a shallow sink of cold water (running water can bruise them) before using.*

778 kj
Fat 2.8 g
Saturated fat 1.0 g
Carbohydrates 32.6 g
Protein 6.5 g
Sugars 21.8 g
Fibre 3.2 g

PER SERVE

RICOTTA & HONEY CREPES

These crepes are divine!

SERVES 4 | PREPARATION 10 MINUTES | COOKING 30 MINUTES

150 g reduced-fat fresh ricotta

1 lemon, zest finely grated, then cut into wedges

2 tablespoons honey

¾ teaspoon ground cinnamon

¾ cup plain flour

185 ml (¾ cup) skim milk

1 egg

olive oil spray

Combine the ricotta, lemon zest, 1 tablespoon honey and ½ teaspoon cinnamon in a bowl, then set aside.

Sift the flour into another bowl. Whisk the milk and egg together in a jug. Add to the flour and whisk until well combined.

Spray a small, non-stick frying pan with oil and heat over medium heat. Pour 2½ tablespoons batter into the pan, swirling the pan around to cover the base. Cook for 2–3 minutes or until light golden, then turn the crepe over and cook for a further 1 minute. Transfer to a clean tea towel. Cover to keep warm. Repeat with the remaining batter.

Spread 1 tablespoon ricotta mixture over each crepe, and roll up to enclose the filling. Drizzle with the remaining honey. Sprinkle with the remaining cinnamon and serve with lemon wedges.

935 kj
Fat 4.7 g
Saturated fat 2.5 g
Carbohydrates 34.3 g
Protein 10.1 g
Sugars 9.6 g
Fibre 1.8 g

PER SERVE

BLUEBERRY MUFFINS

For variety, try other types of berries.

MAKES 12 | PREPARATION 10 MINUTES | COOKING 20 MINUTES

150 g fresh or frozen blueberries
1½ cups rolled oats
1 cup wholemeal self-raising flour
⅓ cup self-raising flour
250 ml (1 cup) apple juice
60 ml (¼ cup) vegetable oil
½ cup honey
1 egg

Preheat oven to 180°C or 160°C fan-forced. Line a 12-hole 80-ml (⅓-cup) muffin tray with paper cases.

In a large mixing bowl, mix together the blueberries, oats and self-raising flours. In another bowl, combine the apple juice, oil, honey and egg. Add the flour mixture to the liquid mixture and stir until just combined.

Spoon the muffin mixture into the prepared cases and bake for 15–20 minutes or until golden and cooked through.

930 kj
Fat 6.5 g
Saturated fat 0.9 g
Carbohydrates 36.0 g
Protein 4.0 g
Sugars 15.8 g
Fibre 2.6 g

PER MUFFIN

WATERMELON SALAD WITH GLACÉ GINGER SYRUP

This fruit salad is as delicious as it is pleasing to the eye.

SERVES 4 | PREPARATION 15 MINUTES + COOLING TIME | COOKING 5 MINUTES

⅓ cup caster sugar

115 g glacé ginger, thinly sliced

1 small seedless watermelon, rind removed, cut into thin wedges

½ cup mint leaves, finely shredded

¼ cup pistachio kernels, thinly sliced

Combine 125 ml (½ cup) water, the sugar and ginger in a small saucepan over low heat. Cook, stirring occasionally, for 2 minutes or until the sugar dissolves. Increase the heat to medium and bring to the boil. Cook for 2 minutes or until the syrup thickens slightly. Set aside for 15 minutes to cool, then place in the fridge for 30 minutes to chill.

Place the watermelon in a large bowl and pour over the cold ginger syrup. Add the mint and gently toss to combine. Divide among serving bowls and sprinkle with pistachios to serve.

TIP *As a variation, make the watermelon salad with a kaffir lime syrup. Replace the glacé ginger with 4 kaffir lime leaves, finely shredded. Omit the mint and replace the pistachio kernels with ¼ cup unsalted macadamia nuts, thinly sliced.*

1537 kj
Fat 7.5 g
Saturated fat 1.4 g
Carbohydrates 68.6 g
Protein 5.4 g
Sugars 66.6 g
Fibre 6.6 g

PER SERVE

BANANA SPLIT

Bananas are a good source of fibre and potassium.

SERVES 4 | PREPARATION 5 MINUTES | COOKING NIL

2 firm ripe bananas

4 small scoops low-fat vanilla ice cream

2 passionfruit, halved

Cut each banana in half lengthwise and place a banana half in the base of four serving dishes.

Top each with a scoop of vanilla ice cream, then spoon the pulp of half a passionfruit over each scoop of ice cream. Serve immediately.

TIP *For a winter treat you can bake the banana by wrapping in foil and baking in a hot oven for 15 to 20 minutes. Unwrap the foil, move the bananas to a serving dish, cool slightly, then top with the ice cream and passionfruit.*

600 kj
Fat 0.9 g
Saturated fat 0.5 g
Carbohydrates 29.0 g
Protein 3.0 g
Sugars 25.3 g
Fibre 3.9 g

PER SERVE

FIG & PECAN BISCOTTI

Be careful not to eat too many – share this crunchy treat over a cuppa with family and friends!

MAKES 24 | PREPARATION 10 MINUTES + COOLING TIME | COOKING 40 MINUTES

⅓ cup caster sugar
1 egg
1 cup (150 g) plain flour
1 teaspoon finely grated lemon zest
⅓ cup chopped dried figs
¼ cup chopped pecan nuts

Preheat oven to 180°c or 160°c fan-forced. Line a large baking tray with baking paper.

Using electric beaters, beat the sugar and egg together for 3 minutes until they have increased in volume and are thick and pale. Sift in the flour and lemon zest and stir with a wooden spoon until almost combined. Add the figs and pecans and, using clean hands, mix until well combined.

Shape the mixture into a log about 24 cm long. Place the log on the prepared tray and flatten slightly to 2 cm thick. Bake for 20 minutes or until firm. Remove from the oven and leave until completely cool.

Reduce the oven temperature to 140°c or 120°c fan-forced. Cut the log using a serrated knife into slices about 8 mm thick. Spread out in a single layer onto the tray and bake for 20 minutes, turning once halfway through the cooking time. Cool completely on wire racks.

TIP *Store in an airtight container for up to 2 weeks.*

220 kj
Fat 1.3 g
Saturated fat 0.1 g
Carbohydrates 9.0 g
Protein 1.2 g
Sugars 4.5 g
Fibre 0.7 g

PER BISCOTTI

BANANA STRUDEL

Everyone will love this delicious dessert, which offers a creative take on the traditional strudel.

SERVES 4 | PREPARATION 15 MINUTES | COOKING 35 MINUTES

- 4 bananas, peeled and thickly sliced
- ⅓ cup sultanas
- 1 tablespoon desiccated coconut
- 2 tablespoons brown sugar
- finely grated zest and juice of 1 orange
- ¾ teaspoon ground cinnamon
- 6 sheets filo pastry
- olive oil spray
- 1 teaspoon caster sugar
- 170 ml (⅓ cup) low-fat vanilla custard, to serve

Preheat oven to 190°C or 170°C fan-forced. Line a baking tray with baking paper.

Place the bananas, sultanas, coconut, brown sugar, orange zest, 2 tablespoons orange juice and ½ teaspoon cinnamon in a bowl. Stir to combine.

Place 1 sheet of filo on a flat work surface. Top with another filo sheet. Spray with oil. Repeat twice with the remaining pastry sheets and oil to make 6 layers.

Spoon the banana mixture along one long edge of the pastry, leaving a 5-cm border on both short ends. Fold the short ends in, then roll up to enclose the filling. Place the strudel, seam side down, on the prepared tray.

Spray the top of the strudel with oil. Combine the caster sugar and remaining ¼ teaspoon cinnamon, and sprinkle over the strudel. Bake for 30–35 minutes or until the pastry is crisp and golden. Stand the strudel on the tray for 5 minutes, then slice and serve with custard.

1189 kj
Fat 3.5 g
Saturated fat 2.3 g
Carbohydrates 35.6 g
Protein 6.2 g
Sugars 39.8 g
Fibre 4.6 g

PER SERVE

TIP *You can replace the banana with 400 g tin pie apple.*

FROZEN FRUIT CRUSH

Let pineapple, orange and passionfruit shine in this light fruit crush.

SERVES 8 | PREPARATION 10 MINUTES + FREEZING TIME | COOKING NIL

1 pineapple, peeled, cored and chopped
2 oranges, peeled and chopped
80 ml (1/3 cup) fresh passionfruit pulp

Place the pineapple, oranges and passionfruit pulp in a food processor and process until smooth. Pour into a large, shallow airtight plastic container. Cover and place in the freezer, mashing with a fork every 3 hours for 10 hours or until set.

To serve, use a fork to scrape the surface into coarse crystals. Divide among serving bowls and serve immediately.

189 kj
Fat 0.1 g
Saturated fat 0.0 g
Carbohydrates 7.8 g
Protein 1.2 g
Sugars 7.8 g
Fibre 3.3 g

PER SERVE

RHUBARB BREAD PUDDINGS

These puddings are a great way to enjoy rhubarb.

SERVES 4 | PREPARATION 20 MINUTES | COOKING 40 MINUTES

1 bunch rhubarb, trimmed and cut into 3 cm pieces
2 tablespoons honey
310 ml (1¼ cups) skim milk
2 eggs
½ teaspoon vanilla essence
8 x 1 cm thick slices baguette bread
¼ teaspoon freshly ground nutmeg

Preheat oven to 180°C or 160°C fan-forced. Place the rhubarb, 1 tablespoon honey and 2 tablespoons cold water in a saucepan over medium heat. Bring to the boil, then cover the pan and cook for 3–5 minutes or until the rhubarb is soft. Allow to cool. Remove ½ cup rhubarb and set aside. Place the remaining rhubarb in a container, cover and refrigerate for another use (see Tip).

Whisk the milk, eggs, vanilla and remaining honey in a bowl until well combined. Press 1 slice of bread into the base of four 185-ml (¾-cup) ramekins. Spoon 2 tablespoons egg mixture over each slice. Top each with 1 tablespoon rhubarb mixture and 1 slice bread. Pour over the remaining egg mixture and sprinkle with nutmeg.

Place the puddings in a roasting tin. Pour boiling water into the tin until the water reaches halfway up the sides of the ramekins. Bake the puddings for 30–35 minutes or until set. Serve warm.

TIP *Stewed rhubarb is also delicious spooned over breakfast cereals such as muesli.*

980 kj
Fat 3.7 g
Saturated fat 1.2 g
Carbohydrates 32.0 g
Protein 13.1 g
Sugars 21.5 g
Fibre 6.2 g

PER SERVE

PEAR FILO TARTS

These tarts look impressive, but come together in no time at all.

SERVES 4 | PREPARATION 25 MINUTES | COOKING 8 MINUTES

8 sheets filo pastry
olive oil spray
2 pears, thinly sliced
2 tablespoons sugar
1 teaspoon ground cardamom
¼ cup slivered almonds
1 tablespoon honey
½ cup low-fat vanilla yoghurt

Preheat oven to 220°C or 200°C fan-forced. Place 1 sheet of filo pastry on a flat work surface and cover the remaining sheets with a dry tea towel, then a damp tea towel (this will prevent the filo from drying out). Lightly spray the filo with oil. Top with another sheet of filo and spray with oil. Fold the pastry in half crosswise. Working quickly, tuck the corners of the pastry under and gently scrunch the pastry to make a wrinkled round. Lift onto a large baking tray. Repeat with the remaining filo sheets to make 3 more rounds.

Place the pear slices into the centres of the pastry rounds. Combine the sugar and cardamom in a small bowl, and sprinkle over the pears and pastry. Spray lightly with oil, then sprinkle with the almonds.

Bake the tarts for 8 minutes or until crisp and golden. Drizzle with honey and serve with yoghurt.

1063 kj
Fat 5.2 g
Saturated fat 0.7 g
Carbohydrates 45.5 g
Protein 6.1 g
Sugars 27.9 g
Fibre 2.9 g

PER SERVE

PASSIONFRUIT SOUFFLÉS

Low in fat and so easy to make!

SERVES 4 | PREPARATION 20 MINUTES | COOKING 20 MINUTES

10 passionfruit, or ½ cup canned pulp, strained to remove seeds

olive oil spray

¾ cup caster sugar

5 eggwhites

853 kj
Fat 0.1 g
Saturated fat 0.0 g
Carbohydrates 42.5 g
Protein 5.8 g
Sugars 15.9 g
Fibre 6.3 g

PER SERVE

Preheat oven to 200°C.

If using fresh passionfruit, remove seeds and pulp. Pass half the amount through a sieve, reserving juice and discarding seeds.

Heat remaining seeds, juice and sugar in a saucepan over low heat and cook, stirring, until thickened.

Spray 4 individual (1-cup capacity) ramekins lightly with oil, then sprinkle with a small amount of caster sugar, ensuring that the base and sides are lightly coated.

Whisk eggwhites until they begin to thicken. Add the sugar slowly while whisking and continue until soft peaks form. Gently fold the passionfruit through, reserving a little of the syrup.

Spoon mixture into ramekins, leaving 1 cm at the top. Bake in the oven for 15–20 minutes until the soufflés have risen and are golden brown.

Drizzle with the reserved passionfruit syrup and serve.

PEAR & COCONUT SPRING ROLLS

A sweet twist on an old favourite.

SERVES 4 | PREPARATION 15 MINUTES | COOKING 10 MINUTES

3 cups (650 g) canned pears

½ cup shredded coconut

½ cup wheatgerm

6 sheets filo pastry

olive oil spray

2 tablespoons brown sugar

Place pears in a mixing bowl and combine with the coconut and wheatgerm.

Place 1 sheet of filo on a flat surface, covering the others to prevent them drying out. Spray the sheet lightly with oil and fold in half. Spray lightly again and sprinkle over a small amount of the brown sugar.

Spoon a sixth of the fruit mixture evenly along the bottom edge of the filo square and roll the square up tightly, spraying lightly with oil to finish and seal. Repeat for the remaining sheets.

Heat a large frying pan over a medium heat and spray lightly with oil. Cut the spring rolls in half and cook for 2 minutes on each side until golden brown. Serve hot.

1088 kj
Fat 7.2 g
Saturated fat 5.6 g
Carbohydrates 40.0 g
Protein 6.0 g
Sugars 30.5 g
Fibre 6.9 g

PER SERVE

SCRUNCHY APPLE PIE

Kids of all ages will enjoy making this fun, fruity pie – and they'll love eating it, too!

SERVES 4 | PREPARATION 20 MINUTES + COOLING TIME | COOKING 25 MINUTES

4 large Granny Smith apples, peeled, cored and cut into thick wedges
1 tablespoon caster sugar
pinch of ground cinnamon
4 sheets filo pastry, cut in half crosswise
olive oil spray
icing sugar mixture, to dust
cream, to serve

683 kj
Fat 1.3 g
Saturated fat 0.6 g
Carbohydrates 35.0 g
Protein 2.1 g
Sugars 26.5 g
Fibre 4.0 g

PER SERVE

Preheat oven to 190°C or 170°C fan-forced. Place the apples and 1 tablespoon water in a large saucepan over high heat and bring to the boil. Reduce the heat to low and cook, covered, for 10 minutes or until the apple softens. Remove the pan from the heat and stir in the sugar and cinnamon. Set aside for 30 minutes to cool.

Spoon the apple mixture into a 1.25-litre (5-cup) ovenproof dish. Place the filo on a clean work surface. Cover with a dry tea towel, then a damp tea towel (this will prevent the filo from drying out). Lightly spray 1 sheet of filo with oil. Fold in half crosswise and scrunch into a rosette shape. Place on top of the apple mixture. Repeat with the remaining filo sheets.

Bake for 15 minutes or until golden. Dust with icing sugar and serve with cream.

PAVLOVA ROLL

A deliciously light treat that everyone will enjoy.

SERVES 10 | PREPARATION 20 MINUTES | COOKING 15 MINUTES

4 eggwhites
½ cup caster sugar
1 teaspoon cornflour
½ teaspoon white vinegar
icing sugar, for dusting
200 g low-fat vanilla fromage frais
250 g strawberries, hulled and halved

Preheat the oven to 180°C. Line a 26 cm x 32 cm Swiss roll pan with baking paper.

Using an electric mixer, beat the eggwhites until soft peaks form. Add the sugar, 1 tablespoon at a time, until all the sugar is incorporated and the meringue is thick and glossy. Beat in the cornflour and vinegar. Spoon the meringue into the prepared pan, gently smoothing the surface with a metal spatula. Bake for 12–15 minutes until the surface is puffed and lightly golden.

Turn the pavlova roll out onto a clean tea towel that has been lightly dusted with icing sugar. Peel away the baking paper and with the long side facing you, carefully roll up, using the tea towel as a guide. Set aside to cool.

When the pavlova is completely cool, unroll it and spread with the fromage frais, leaving a 2-cm border around the edges. Top with the strawberries and re-roll. Slice and serve.

302 kj
Fat 0.0 g
Saturated fat 0.0 g
Carbohydrates 14.0 g
Protein 3.5 g
Sugars 13.5 g
Fibre 0.6 g

PER SERVE

VANILLA-POACHED NASHI PEARS

Also known as Asian pears, nashi have a crisp juicy flesh that is delicious eaten raw or poached.

SERVES 4 | PREPARATION 10 MINUTES + 10 MINUTES INFUSING | COOKING 15 MINUTES

2 vanilla beans

½ cup caster sugar

1 cinnamon stick

2 pieces of orange peel

4 nashi pears, peeled

Use a sharp paring knife to split the vanilla beans lengthways and scrape out the seeds. Place seeds and split beans in a medium saucepan with three cups of water, sugar, cinnamon and orange peel. Stir over a low heat until the sugar has dissolved.

Add the nashi pears to the pan and increase the heat to medium. Simmer, covered, for 10 minutes, or until the nashi pears are tender. Remove the pan from the heat and leave for 10 minutes for the flavours to infuse.

Serve the poached nashi pears warm or cold, drizzled with syrup.

752 kj
Fat 0.2 g
Saturated fat 0.0 g
Carbohydrates 44.0 g
Protein 0.7 g
Sugars 43.6 g
Fibre 2.6 g

PER SERVE

Index

N

O

P

R

S

T

V

HOUSEHOLD WEIGHTS AND MEASURES

Teaspoons, tablespoons, cups

1 Australian metric teaspoon = 5ml/5g
1 Australian metric tablespoon = 20ml/20g
1 Australian metric cup = 250ml
3 tablespoons = ¼ cup
4 tablespoons = ⅓ cup

OVEN TEMPERATURES	°C (CELSIUS)	°F (FAHRENHEIT)
Very Slow	120	250
Slow	150	300
Moderately Slow	160	325
Moderate	180	350
Moderately Hot	190	375
Hot	200	400
Very Hot	220-250	450-500

Published in 2012 by Hardie Grant Books

Hardie Grant Books (Australia)
Ground Floor, Building 1
658 Church Street
Richmond, Victoria 3121
www.hardiegrant.com.au

Hardie Grant Books (UK)
Dudley House, North Suite
34–35 Southampton Street
London WC2E 7HF
www.hardiegrant.co.uk

Cataloguing-in-Publication data is available from the National Library of Australia.
The Biggest Loser: 100 Healthy Desserts
ISBN 9 781742704043

Additional material provided by NewsLifeMedia: Emma Braz, Claire Brookman, Kerrie Butler , Kim Coverdale, Veronica Cuskelly, Teresa Cutter, Dixie Elliott, Annette Forrest, Chrissy Freer, Sarah Hobbs, Kirrily La Rosa, Gemma Luongo, Kim Meredith, Michelle Noerianto, Louise Pickford, Jan Purser, Alison Roberts, Tracy Rutherford, Michelle Southan, Rosemary Stanton, Kerrie Sun , Abi Ulgiati.

Nutrition Consultant: Dr Trent Watson

Colour reproduction by Splitting Image Colour Studio

Printed and bound in China by 1010 Printing International Limited